COUSIN RICK'S
Game & Fish
COOKBOOK

RICK BLACK

STACKPOLE
BOOKS
Guilford, Connecticut

To my son, Travis, and his beautiful wife, Erica. God blessed me and Becky on the day you were born and again with Gavin (GW) and Mason and Evelin (the twins), who all stole our hearts. Even as a seasoned author, I cannot put down in words my pride and love. I truly cherish our hunts together and watching you use your outdoor cooking skills and being a chip off the old block. You have been the perfect son and are now the perfect husband, father, and citizen.

Also, I want to say goodbye to baby girl Princess, our beloved little Yorkie that we lost in December of 2017. Of all the dogs we have had for home and field, baby girl was the light of our lives. This little critter will be deeply missed.

Love, Pop

Published by Stackpole Books
An imprint of The Rowman & Littlefield Publishing Group, Inc.
4501 Forbes Blvd., Ste. 200
Lanham, MD 20706
www.rowman.com

Distributed by NATIONAL BOOK NETWORK
800-462-6420

Cartoons by Dan Roberts

British Library Cataloguing in Publication Information available

Library of Congress Cataloging-in-Publication Data available

ISBN 978-0-8117-3824-8 (hardcover)
ISBN 978-0-8117-6825-2 (e-book)

♾™ The paper used in this publication meets the minimum requirements of American National Standard for Information Sciences—Permanence of Paper for Printed Library Materials, ANSI/NISO Z39.48-1992.

CONTENTS

ACKNOWLEDGMENTS

This book would not have been possible without years of hunting with some of the very best people on earth. I have been truly blessed for this. Thank you to Sparky Sparks and the great team at M2D (Made to Deceive) Camo; I cannot think of a hunting or fishing trip where I did not have my M2D camo and gear. To Judith and Stephanie at Stackpole Books. To Uncle Ted Nugent, for inspiring me to write the crazy things that pop into my head under that camp cap I wear. To Jim Ferguson from the Great American Outdoor Trails Radio Show. To Dan Roberts, my wonderful illustrator and good friend. To Jeff and Linda May, for being lifelong friends and for allowing me to hunt with them on their perfect Iowa land. I would also like to thank my parents, whose love and guidance are with me in whatever I pursue. They were the ultimate role models. Most importantly, I wish to thank my loving and supportive wife, Becky, and my wonderful son, Travis, who both provide unending inspiration. Finally, I want to thank all my fans and loyal readers, whom I truly enjoy talking to at book signings, hunts, and outdoor cooking events.

INTRODUCTION

After the successes of my previous wild game and outdoor cooking books, I wanted to write the granddaddy of all wild game cookbooks—this one.

Cooking with wild game will always be a passion of mine. I cherish every aspect of it, starting with the hunt itself. I have had people tell me at book signings and on the radio, "I got a freezer full of wild game, and I didn't have to set foot into the timber or blind to get it." To those folks I quickly reply, "I'm sorry about your luck!"

My theory is there's a big difference in how an outdoorsman cooks and how a wild game meal tastes when you are the one who brought the game home. The planning, scouting, shot, and hooking (and of course the pride and bragging rights) all play a major role in the art of wild game cooking.

My goal for this book is to share many of my favorite wild game recipes and to write the most complete wild game book out there, something any hunter and outdoorsman can cherish for years to come. I've also included outstanding tips on hunting and preparing wild game, as well as a few funnies and some great illustrations. I truly believe this is my best work ever, and I am excited to share this with you, my loyal readers and my new ones too.

Wild Game Cooking Safety

As I have written in previous books, great tasting wild game starts with the field dressing and cleaning of the game. Always go the extra mile to have a well-cleaned harvest.

Safely harvesting wild game is the first step to flavor. To reduce the likelihood of any bacterial disease, it's also critical to thoroughly cook wild game meat. Be sure to cook the meat until it is no longer pink and the juices run clear.

Here are some of my other tips for safe handling of your wild game:

- Hunters should NEVER handle or consume wild animals that appear sick or act abnormally.
- Always wear heavy rubber or latex gloves when field dressing your wild game.
- Handle carcasses properly by cooling the carcass rapidly in the field if possible. (Bags of ice or snow can hasten cooling.) Hold meat at or below 40 degrees Fahrenheit at all times. Age the carcass for no longer than 5 to 7 days. Hang birds by the feet for 2 to 3 days maximum.
- If the intestinal contents contact the meat, the meat is contaminated; cut off and discard the affected area.
- If you don't plan to consume or process the meat within 3 to 5 days, freeze it. Thaw frozen meat only in the refrigerator, never at room temperature.

COUSIN RICK'S MEASURING TIPS

As we continue our wild game cooking adventure, I wanted to take a few minutes to give you a guide to cooking measurements. This is a very good tool, and you will want to refer back to it often.

Gallon: gal
Ounce: oz.

Pint: pt.
Quart: qt.

Tablespoon: Tbls.
Teaspoon: tsp.

1 tsp. = $\frac{1}{3}$ Tbls. or $\frac{1}{63}$ cup or $\frac{1}{6}$ oz.

2 tsp. = $\frac{2}{3}$ Tbls. or $\frac{1}{32}$ cup or $\frac{1}{3}$ oz.

3 tsp. = 1 Tbls. or $\frac{1}{16}$ cup or $\frac{1}{2}$ oz.

6 tsp. = 2 Tbls. or $\frac{1}{8}$ cup or 1 oz.

12 tsp. = 4 Tbls. or $\frac{1}{4}$ cup or 2 oz.

16 tsp. = $5\frac{1}{2}$ Tbls. or $\frac{1}{3}$ cup or $2\frac{2}{3}$ oz.

24 tsp. = 8 Tbls. or $\frac{1}{2}$ cup or 4 oz.

32 tsp. = $10\frac{2}{3}$ Tbls. or $\frac{2}{3}$ cup or $5\frac{1}{3}$ oz.

36 tsp. = 12 Tbls. or $\frac{3}{4}$ cup or 6 oz.

48 tsp. = 16 Tbls. or 1 cup or 8 oz.

1 cup = $\frac{1}{2}$ pt. or $\frac{1}{4}$ qt. or $\frac{1}{16}$ gal. or 8 oz.

2 cups = 1 pt. or $\frac{1}{2}$ qt. or $\frac{1}{8}$ gal. or 16 oz.

3 cups = $1\frac{1}{2}$ pt. or $\frac{3}{4}$ qt. or $\frac{3}{16}$ gal. or 24 oz.

4 cups = 2 pt. or 1 qt. or $\frac{1}{4}$ gal. or 32 oz.

5 cups = $2\frac{1}{2}$ pt. or $1\frac{1}{4}$ qt. or $\frac{5}{16}$ gal. or 40 oz.

6 cups = 3 pt. or $1\frac{1}{2}$ qt. or $\frac{3}{8}$ gal. or 48 oz.

8 cups = 4 pt. or 2 qt. or $\frac{1}{2}$ gal. or 64 oz.

10 cups = 5 pt. or $2\frac{1}{2}$ qt. or $\frac{5}{8}$ gal. or 80 oz.

12 cups = 6 pt. or 3 qt. or $\frac{3}{4}$ gal. or 96 oz.

16 cups = 8 pt. or 4 qt. or 1 gal. or 128 oz.

- Wash your hands with soap and warm water before and after handling wild game meat.
- Sanitize your equipment and work surfaces often during handling and processing; use a bleach solution of 1 tablespoon of bleach to 1 gallon of water.
- Always use a meat thermometer to cook your game to the correct temperature. There are several types available, all of which are easy to use and can be read instantly or remain in the meat while it cooks. This helps you ensure that harmful bacteria are killed and that the meat is not overcooked. The color of meat is not a reliable indicator of doneness. At the very least, always cook the game meat until no longer pink and the juices run clear.

Cooking Methods

Whether you choose to cook wild game directly or indirectly usually depends on the game meat to be cooked. In fact, I often combine both methods of cooking when I chose to barbecue my game.

Direct Cooking

The food is cooked directly above the heat source. This method is perfect for fast-cooking game like deer burger, chops, steaks, and fish fillets.

Indirect Cooking

A good example of indirect cooking would be to build a fire in one half of the grill, and place your game meat on the opposite side of the cooking grid, away from the heat. Perfect for large cuts of meats, fowl sections, and large game ribs.

Dry Smoking

Dry smoking can be done on almost every type of covered grill. Place the game on a grid above the coals, and then cover the grill with a lid. The lid concentrates the smoke around the game meat, which permeates the meat with a strong smoke flavor depending on the wood chips you use. Of course, while any grill will work, I highly recommend a quality smoker if you want to ensure success.

Water Smoking

Charcoal water smoking works just like dry smoking, except a pan of water (or another liquid, such as beer) is placed between the coals and the rack holding the food. The game meat cooks very slowly in a dense cloud of smoke and steam from the liquid. This makes for wonderfully tasting, moist and tender game.

Cast Iron Cooking

Using a skillet, Dutch oven, or griddle.

COUSIN RICK'S TIPS ON HOW TO SEASON A DUTCH OVEN

There are many different ways to season a Dutch oven, but they all have a few things in common. The objective is to bake a coating of oil onto the surface of the oven, which has several benefits: It prevents the metal from rusting and creates a nonstick surface that makes cleanup easier, plus it adds a delicious, subtle flavor unmatched by other types of cookware.

When you purchase a new Dutch oven, it comes from the foundry with a thin waxy coating designed to prevent rusting until the oven can be properly seasoned. This coating will be washed off, with any residue burned off during the seasoning process.

Here are some tips I picked up from the pros:

1. Peel off any labels, and then warm the Dutch oven.

2. Wash, rinse, and dry the pot. Grease inside lightly with solid shortening.

3. Bake at 300 degrees in a conventional oven for 1 hour. (Don't be alarmed by the smoke that will come from your oven as the shortening is burned onto the metal surface of the Dutch oven. Open your doors and windows, and make sure to temporarily turn off the smoke alarm.)

4. After the Dutch oven has cooled, wipe out any excess grease. Store the oven with a paper towel inside, with the edges of the towel hanging out from under the lid to absorb any excess oils and to allow air to enter the oven.

5. Repeat this process if part of the oven did not season properly.

Over time, your Dutch oven will develop a hard, smooth, black coating on its inside. When you reach this point, you will truly have a "seasoned" oven that you'll never want to part with. And of course, this will make you the master of wild game cooking!

Pellet Grill/Smoker Tips and Tricks

Pellet smokers are wood-fired smokers that burn compressed wood—called "pellets"—as the sole heat source. They allow you to cook at precise temperatures and are very versatile, meaning they're perfect for wild game whether you're cooking low and slow or grilling at high heat. My wife, Mrs. Becky, even uses our smoker for baking. These efficient, simple grills have been around for a long time, but nowadays, they've become the "cool" way to cook at camp and yes, even at barbecue competitions.

My grill is easy to use. It has a hopper that holds pellets, and in the bottom of that hopper is an auger that moves the pellets slowly into the fire box. This is where they burn, producing heat and smoke for cooking. The whole cooker is run by a built-in control panel that is basically the boss of the smoker. Set the temp, and the unit starts dropping pellets into the fire box, where a heating probe starts the fire. There's no messing with a flame, lighter fluid, or anything else. This gives you a mild, clean smoke throughout the entire cook—the cooker does the work for you. If you can down a 12-pointer, you can fire up this simple smoker.

WHEN DOES A CRITTER NEED TO BE AGED?

Aging times for poultry are not in days but in hours. Most large animals will be aged in 14 days. Young animals are tender by nature, and a suckling pig or veal doesn't need to be aged. By the time most meat is brought back from the hunt, the aging is completed. Operations like chopping or mechanically grinding tenderize meat, and hunters who grind their meat don't have to worry about aging it. Game that is killed at 65 degrees or above and held at this temperature for 1 day should be processed immediately. The same meat killed at 34 degrees will have to be aged for 2 weeks. The best way to preserve wild game is by freezing. Freeze and store game meat at 0 degrees or lower. Frozen meat will keep up to one year without loss of quality.

Barbecue Is a Man's Job

After four long months of winter, we are finally coming up on barbecue season. So let me tell you our routine when Becky and I decide to fire up the grill on a Saturday night:

1) Becky buys the food. (Cousin Rick has had a tough season.)

2) Becky makes the salad, prepares the vegetables, and makes dessert.

3) Becky prepares the meat for cooking, places it on a tray along with the necessary cooking utensils and sauces, and takes it to Cousin Rick, who is lounging beside the grill, drink in hand.

4) COUSIN RICK PLACES THE MEAT ON THE GRILL.

5) Becky goes inside to organize the plates and cutlery.

6) Becky comes out to tell Cousin Rick that the meat is burning. He thanks her and asks if she will bring another drink while he deals with the situation.

7) COUSIN RICK TAKES THE MEAT OFF THE GRILL AND HANDS IT TO HIS WIFE.

8) Becky prepares the plates, salad, bread, utensils, napkins, and sauces and then brings them to the table.

9) Everyone eats, then Becky clears the table and does the dishes.

10) Everyone PRAISES Cousin Rick and THANKS HIM for his heroic cooking efforts.

11) Cousin Rick asks Becky how she enjoyed her night off, and, upon seeing her annoyed reaction, concludes that there's just no pleasing some women.

UNCLE RONNIE'S PLAQUE

Growing up in southeast Iowa on the banks of the Mississippi, I had the privilege of outstanding hunting, fishing, and trapping. With most of my family living in the Midwest, as I grew older I got to hunt in Michigan, Minnesota, Illinois, Missouri, Wisconsin, and South Dakota. I grew up on fish, duck, pheasant, small game, and big game. My uncle Ronnie was a fish cop in northern Iowa (with the Department of Natural Resources), and I remember a wooden plaque he had that, as young outdoorsmen, my cousin and I had to read before every hunting and fishing trip with him. I want to share the words with you, so in return you can keep this pledge going.

The future of the sport of hunting, fishing, and trapping depends on each hunter's behavior and ethics. Therefore, as an outdoorsman, I pledge to do the following:

Respect the environment and wildlife.
- Show respect for the wildlife you hunt by taking only clean, killing shots, then retrieving and properly handing your game. Take only what you will use, even if it is under the legal limit.
- Learn to tread lightly while afield. Use vehicles only on established roads and trails, practice low-impact camping and travel, and pack out your trash, including spent shell casings.
- Report signs of illegal activities immediately to the game warden, Department of Natural Resources, and police.

Respect property and landowners.
- Always get permission to fish or hunt on private land.
- Close any gates you open, and never damage crops or property, including fences, docks, outbuildings, and livestock.
- Alert landowners or land managers about any problems you find on their property.
- Share your fish and game with the landowner, or say thank you in some other way.

Show consideration for non-outdoorsmen.
- Remember that the future of hunting depends on hunters and non-hunters alike. Be considerate of non-hunters' sensibilities, and strive to leave them with positive images of hunting and hunters.
- Do not flaunt your kill. Treat game carcasses in a respectful manner, particularly during transport.
- Be considerate of all outdoor users, including other hunters and fishermen.

Hunt and fish safely.
- Exercise caution at all times.
- Fire your gun or bow only when you are absolutely sure of your target and its background. Use binoculars, not your scope, to identify your target.

- Wear blaze orange whenever appropriate or required afield by state law.
- Remember that fishing, hunting, and alcohol don't mix.

Know and obey the law.
- Obtain proper tags and license.
- Hunt and fish only in allowed areas and during designated times and seasons.
- Read hunting, fishing, and trapping regulations carefully.
- Obey bag and possession limits.
- Use only legal hunting, fishing, and trapping methods and equipment.

Support wildlife and habitat conservation.
- Provide hands-on and financial support for conservation of game and non-game species and their habitats.
- Learn more about wildlife and habitat issues, and urge policymakers to support strong conservation initiatives.
- Become involved in wildlife conservation organizations and the programs they represent.
- Purchase state and federal wildlife conservation stamps, even if such stamps are not required for hunting and fishing.

Pass on an ethical sportsman tradition.
- Invite a young person or a non-hunter the next time you go afield to scout or hunt.
- Attend a hunter education course, and urge others to do the same.
- Set high ethical standards for future generations of outdoorsmen to help ensure our sport will continue.

Strive to improve outdoor skills and understanding of fish and game.
- Know the limitations of your skills and equipment, and hunt and fish within those limits.
- Improve your outdoor skills to become more observant, a better hunter, and a better teacher.
- Sight in your firearm and bow, and practice shooting to ensure a clean kill in the field.
- Learn more about the habits and habitats of game and non-game wildlife and fish, as well as their management needs.

Fish and hunt only with ethical sportsmen.
- Take pride in being an ethical hunter and fisherman
- Insist that your outdoor partners behave in a responsible, ethical manner.
- Compete only with yourself.

By following these principles of conduct each time I go to field and stream, I will give my best to the sport, the public, the environment, and myself. The responsibility to hunt and fish ethically is mine: the future of hunting and fishing depends on me!

FOOD SAFETY OF WILD GAME

Store-bought or commercial meat is chilled rapidly, but game meat such as venison is often kept at higher-than-recommended temperatures, which may create conditions for the growth of bacteria. The safety of the meat can be affected by the location of the wound and the processing skills of the hunter. If the animal is wounded or cut during slaughtering in such a way that the contents of its gut come in contact with the meat or hands of the operator, fecal bacteria can contaminate the meat. That's why when you're field dressing an animal, you need to stay away from that gut sack.

Wild game such as deer and bear are often infected with the trichina parasite, which is destroyed at 137 degrees. If present in pork, this parasite may also be destroyed by keeping meat frozen. My dad and uncles taught me that meat coming from wild animals living in cold climates is resilient to cold treatment for trichinae, and the only way to be safe is to cook the meat to an internal temperature of 160 degrees. Questions about game meat condition are hard to answer unless the hunter processes the meat himself. With store-bought game, you know the meat has been inspected by the state or federal meat inspectors.

The sooner the animal is dressed after shooting, the better the quality of the meat will be. If the weather is hot, removing the skin will facilitate cooling. The critter will have to be wrapped in cheesecloth and dressed with black pepper to protect it from flies. If the weather is cold, it is better to leave the skin on to prevent the meat from drying and keep the carcass clean.

"I told you it was too cold for hunting."

CHAPTER 1

Wild Game and Fish Marinades, Sauces, Rubs, and Brines

I have said it before, and I will say it again: If you're going to cook wild game and fish, the trick is in the marinades, sauces, rubs, and brines.

Marinades

I was asked a few years ago why I was so dang fussy about using marinades. Probably the number-one reason to use marinade with game and fish is for the flavor. You have the freedom to choose ingredients that suit your taste—including herbs, seasonings, and spices—giving you limitless possibilities to customize the flavor.

The acid in the marinade chemically alters the muscle fibers, giving game meat a more tender texture. Since the acids you'll use include vinegar, wine, beer, lemon juice, and lime juice, they also have a great influence on the flavor. I try to keep my marinade recipes simple, in that they only contain an acid, oil, and seasonings. OK, maybe some of my marinade recipes for game and fish can have a pretty long list of ingredients (seasonings, spices, and such), and sometimes I do tend to go overboard (like some of my barbecue rub recipes).

Marinating times vary from a few minutes to 24 hours. A combination of factors figure into how long the marinating should last. Type of game meat, size of the game meat, delicateness, strength of the acid, and temperature are some things to consider. For example, small pieces of bluegill or catfish in lime juice at room temperature would only need a few minutes to marinate. On the other hand, a 4-pound deer brisket in soy sauce in the refrigerator might need to marinate overnight or longer. Of course you still have to be careful and follow some basic food safety practices when using marinade recipes too. Clean surfaces thoroughly, and avoid excess contamination. Throw out any leftover marinade that has come into contact with raw meat. And always marinate in the refrigerator or a cooler.

I remember learning in school that in ancient times hunters tried different ways to preserve meat. If you remember from history class, refrigerators didn't work back then (no place to plug them in—ha!). They tried salt, sun, and other ways of drying the meat. So today my marinade recipes are fairly standard (acid, oil, seasonings). But that's far from saying "they're all alike." You have the power to make them taste the way you want, brother. Delete, add, or adjust ingredients to suit your own taste. You will get better with practice (really!). Take advantage of all those centuries of experimentation, and try it: Get yourself another cold brew dog and create a marinade. Let's get started!

AL AND MARGE SAUTNER'S MARINADE FOR ELK

1 teaspoon ginger

1 teaspoon dry mustard

¾ cup extra virgin olive oil

3 well-pressed garlic cloves

½ cup soy sauce

1 tablespoon molasses

In a large bowl, mix together the ginger, dry mustard, olive oil, garlic, soy sauce, and molasses. Cover the elk meat, and marinate in the refrigerator for a minimum of 24 hours. This marinade not only tenderizes the meat but will also add flavor and remove any strong game taste. I have used this recipe on mule deer and had the satisfaction of a very tasty roast.

PRAIRIE CHICKEN TERIYAKI MARINADE

½ cup mirin (a heavily sweetened sake)

⅓ cup soy sauce

3 tablespoons sugar

1 tablespoon grated ginger

1 minced garlic clove

In a glass bowl, mix together all the ingredients, and then store the mixture in a cooler or refrigerator. Use as a marinade on your prairie chicken. This also makes a great marinade for duck and quail.

The Boys I Fish With!

A funeral service passes over the bridge where Bubba and I were fishing, and Bubba takes off his hat and puts it over his heart.

I said, "Gee Bubba, I didn't know you had it in you!"

Bubba replied, "It's the least I could do. After all, I was married to her for 30 years."

WILD GAME GARLIC MARINADE

1½ cups salad oil

¾ cup soy sauce

¼ cup Worcestershire sauce

2 tablespoons dry mustard

1 tablespoon ground black pepper

½ cup apple cider vinegar

2 tablespoons parsley

2 cloves garlic

Place all the ingredients together in a large blender, and mix well on high speed. Marinate the game overnight, keeping some of the marinade for basting if on the grill.

HUNTER ISLAND SEAFOOD MARINADE

1 (12-ounce) can of beer

¾ cup fresh lime juice

6 garlic cloves, minced

1 teaspoon chicken bouillon

1 tablespoon Worcestershire sauce

1 tablespoon black pepper

1 yellow onion, finely chopped

Whisk all ingredients in a large bowl to blend. Let this marinade stand for about an hour before using. Covered in the refrigerator, the marinade will last about a week. This is a must-have for your favorite catch, and I whip it up at every fishing trip.

"I bagged my first lawn ornament of the season."

©2016 Dan Roberts

Sauces

TODD LARSON'S BOURBON SAUCE FOR PHEASANT

2 tablespoons salted butter

2 tablespoons minced onion

2 garlic cloves, minced

6 ounces tomato paste

½ cup Kentucky bourbon

½ cup water

¼ cup packed brown sugar

2 tablespoons Worcestershire sauce

½ teaspoon basil

½ teaspoon sage

½ teaspoon oregano

1 teaspoon Louisiana Hot Sauce

In a large pan, melt the butter over medium heat. Add the onion and garlic, and then cook until the onion is soft and tender. Stir in the tomato paste, bourbon, water, sugar, Worcestershire sauce, basil, sage, oregano, and Louisiana Hot Sauce. Reduce the heat. Cover and simmer on low for 10 to 15 minutes. Brush this sauce over the pheasant while it cooks. I have also used this outstanding sauce to enhance the flavor of wild turkey breast.

JOSH CLARK'S BBQ SQUIRREL SAUCE

20 ounces Worcestershire sauce

¼ cup vegetable oil

½ cup ketchup

¼ cup white vinegar

¼ cup garlic powder

⅛ tablespoon ground black pepper

½ cup lemon juice

1 (12-ounce) can of cola

Mix all the ingredients together, and simmer for 30 minutes. After simmering, baste them "tree rats" until tender.

WHEN DO I PUT ON MY BARBECUE SAUCE?

Applying Barbecue Sauce Too Early

Some outdoor cooks may coat their protein with the barbecue sauce before even putting it on the hot grill. Others wait until the game meat starts to cook, but they don't wait long enough, basting too early in the cooking process. This will not end well, and it's all due to a specific ingredient in barbecue sauce: sugar.

As you will see in this chapter, most barbecue sauces contain sugar, which burns at a temperature of about 265 degrees. If you are cooking above this temperature—as you most likely will when you're grilling—then the sugars in your sauce will burn, giving a bad flavor to your hard-earned harvest. The sauce can also turn gummy, creating a strange texture to the game meat. That ain't a good thing!

Applying Barbecue Sauce Too Late

The other school of thought is to wait until the vittles come off the grill to coat with sauce. That means that the meat or game bird doesn't have the chance to absorb any of the delicious flavors of the sauce while cooking, when its ability to soak in flavors is at its peak. I didn't work my tail off giving you great barbecue sauce recipes for you to mess up them tasty critters!

(This does not apply to sauces that are used to flavor barbecue as it cooks. Thick barbecue sauces should be held off for later for the sake of flavor, not because they will burn on the meat.)

Applying Barbecue Sauce at the Right Time

So, when is the perfect time to baste your game meat with barbecue sauce?

That would be when the meat is about 10 minutes away from being done. You want to give the sauce enough heat to begin to caramelize, which will add a rich flavor, but not so much heat that it starts to burn. Begin brushing on the sauce, adding two or three more coats until you remove the meat from the grill. If you notice a flare-up, move the meat to a cooler part of the grill.

Game ribs, however, can handle sauce applied earlier in the cooking process. Most of the hicks I hunt with expect a thick barbecue sauce on their venison and buffalo ribs, so you should layer it on during the last 30 to 60 minutes of cooking. Apply several thin coatings to build layers. This is what makes for a sticky, delicious surface on them tasty ribs.

Applying Barbecue Sauce When Smoking

Since smoking is typically done at much lower temperatures than grilling, you don't have to worry about the sauce burning and ruining your grub. You may get some caramelization of the sugar, which will deepen the longer it is on, but it won't burn and cause you any real problems.

The Best Way Is on the Side

In true barbecue, most meat is served with barbecue sauce as a condiment, not as an ingredient. Whether you baste the meat while on the grill or serve the sauce on the side, the flavors you add to grilled and smoked game meats should be controlled. Make the most of your barbecue by allowing the hungry hunters to add sauce if desired.

FLOYD BLACK'S MICHIGAN WILD GAME BBQ SAUCE

2 onions, chopped

1 tomato, chopped

2 bay leaves

3 garlic cloves, minced

5 tablespoons salted butter

1½ tablespoons chili powder

1 cup ketchup

½ cup dark amber beer

1 ounce Canadian whiskey

4 tablespoons apple cider vinegar

3 tablespoons packed brown sugar

2 tablespoons prepared mustard

2 tablespoons olive oil

1 teaspoon Frank's RedHot (or similar sauce)

1 teaspoon white pepper

1 orange, sliced

1 teaspoon peanut butter

In a large black iron pot or skillet, cook the onion and garlic in butter until they are tender. Add the remaining ingredients except the orange slices and peanut butter. Bring the sauce to a boil, and then remove from heat. Let the sauce stand for 30 minutes while stirring often with a wooden spoon. Add the orange slices and peanut butter, and simmer on low heat for 5 minutes, again stirring often. Serve this great sauce on all your game. Grandpa developed this sauce for his wild game while living in the great state of Michigan, and he swore that it took the game taste out of black bear. I had the privilege of tasting his cooking and proving him right! This is one of my most-requested and most-used barbecue sauces.

Rubs

VENISON COATING MIX

3 cups flour

1 cup cornmeal

1 teaspoon salt

½ teaspoon ground pepper

2 tablespoons paprika

½ teaspoon garlic powder

1 tablespoon ground turmeric

2 tablespoons thyme

2 tablespoons marjoram

1 tablespoon fresh ground basil

1 tablespoon oregano

1 tablespoon sage

1 tablespoon celery seeds

Combine ingredients, and mix well. Store in an airtight container, and keep frozen or in the refrigerator. I use the seasoned coating on venison loins while frying in butter in a cast iron skillet. This is a favorite with my hunting party. As with all my recipes, you can adjust the seasonings to your taste.

KAHOKA WILD GAME AND CATFISH SEASONING

1 (26-ounce) box of salt

2 ounces fresh ground black pepper

1 ounce red pepper

1 ounce garlic powder

1 ounce chili powder

Mix the salt, ground black pepper, red pepper, garlic powder, and chili powder. Store this seasoning in an airtight container, and use it on your wild game. The first time I tasted this great seasoning was in Kahoka, Missouri, at a volunteer fire department catfish fry fundraiser. The cook also told me that this seasoning is outstanding on turtle, although I have not personally tasted that yet. But I will! Very good stuff.

JEFF MAY'S SLAP HAPPY FISH SPICE

6 tablespoons paprika

¼ cup salt

¼ cup garlic powder

2 tablespoons ground black pepper

2 tablespoons onion powder

2 tablespoons cayenne pepper

2 tablespoons oregano

1 tablespoon thyme

In a glass or stainless bowl, mix together all the ingredients until very well blended. Coat your favorite fish before frying.

SOUTH CAROLINA WILD BOAR RUB

6 tablespoons paprika

2 tablespoons onion powder

2 tablespoons garlic powder

3 tablespoons garlic salt

3 tablespoons smoked salt

2 tablespoons fresh ground black pepper

2 tablespoons sugar

2 tablespoons dried ground basil

2 tablespoons dried ground oregano

2 tablespoons ground thyme

1 teaspoon sage

1 teaspoon dried ground nutmeg

1 teaspoon dried ground ginger

1 teaspoon cumin

1 teaspoon dried ground rosemary

1 teaspoon dried mustard

1 cup minced mint leaves

½ cup packed brown sugar

½ cup Accent Meat Tenderizer

In a large bowl, mix all ingredients together well. Rub the mixture into wild boar meat on all sides at least 12 hours before grilling or smoking.

IOWA WHITETAIL LOIN RUB

4 tablespoons salt

2 tablespoons paprika

1 tablespoon fresh ground black pepper

2 teaspoons onion powder

2 teaspoons garlic powder

2 teaspoons cayenne pepper

½ teaspoon turmeric

½ teaspoon coriander

Mix the ingredients together, and rub them into the deer loins at least 30 minutes before grilling. Good stuff!

WAPELLO FISH RUB

2 teaspoons ground cumin

2 tablespoons ground ginger

2 tablespoons Accent Meat Tenderizer

2 tablespoons ground coriander

1 tablespoon paprika

1 tablespoon sea salt

1 tablespoon cayenne

Mix all ingredients together, and rub them into all sides of your favorite fish. This rub is a great recipe for grilling on the beach or at a cabin.

Brines

COUSIN RICK'S WILD TURKEY BRINE

1½ gallons ice-cold water

1½ cups salt

5 tablespoons finely minced garlic

1 tablespoon fresh ground black pepper

¾ cup Worcestershire sauce

½ cup packed brown sugar

½ pint fresh grapefruit juice (or one can from the store)

Add all ingredients to a plastic food-grade bucket, and mix well. Add the whole wild turkey and cover. Marinate for 48 hours in a cooler or refrigerator. This brine is a winner for smoking or roasting your big Tom gobbler. I have also used this brine for smoking large carp, sturgeon, flathead catfish, and shark.

COUSIN RICK'S WHISKEY RIVER BRINE FOR SMOKING

4 tablespoons butter

¼ cup dark brown sugar

2 tablespoons honey

1 cup water

½ cup fresh apple cider

⅓ cup Worcestershire sauce

¼ cup your favorite whiskey (or bourbon)

2 teaspoons pepper

¼ cup flour

1 quart chicken broth

Mix all the ingredients together in a large bowl or food bucket, and use for smoking fish, duck, turkey, or strong flavor meats like beaver tail or coon. Remember, all brines with game must stay refrigerated.

Funny Fishing Bumper Stickers I Have Seen on the back of Trucks and Boats!

Fishing isn't a sport. It's a condition.

A bad day fishing beats a good day working.

Good things come to those who bait.

Nothing makes a fish bigger than almost being caught.

There are two types of fisherman: those who fish for sport and those who fish for fish.

Fishing is the sport of drowning worms.

Give a man a fish, and he will eat for a day. Teach him how to fish, and he will sit in a boat and drink beer all day.

An angler is a man who spends rainy days sitting around on the muddy banks of rivers doing nothing because his wife won't let him do it at home.

The best way to a fisherman's heart is through his fly.

Even if you've been fishing for three hours and haven't gotten anything except poison ivy and sunburn, you're still better off than the worm.

CHAPTER 2

Wild Fish Cooking: Recipes Using Fish from Sea, Rivers, Lakes, and Ponds

Growing up in southeast Iowa as a kid, I could not imagine any better fishing than on the mighty Mississippi, Lake Keosauqua, the Des Moines River, Skunk River, and my dad's three large stocked ponds. I had it all for fishing and trapping. That was until I had the chance to deep-sea fish in Florida. WOW! This fishing was on a whole new level and led to Alaska salmon fishing and . . . well, you get my drift. Along the way, I had the privilege to cook and eat all the fish harvested, from sleeping bag to lounge, from tent to cabin, and everywhere in between.

The following are my most favorite recipes, and I hope you enjoy them as much as I enjoyed hooking the fish and preparing them for the plate.

The Boys I Fish With!

Bubba: What do you get when you cross a fishing lure with a gym sock?

Cousin Rick: I don't know. What?

Bubba: A hook, line, and stinker!

OTTER CREEK TROUT

¼ cup all-purpose flour

1 tablespoon paprika (plus more for sprinkling)

1 teaspoon dried rosemary (plus more for sprinkling)

1 teaspoon garlic powder (plus more for sprinkling)

1 teaspoon dried parsley (plus more for sprinkling)

1 teaspoon dried dill weed (plus more for sprinkling)

½ teaspoon salt

½ teaspoon ground black pepper

4 whole trout, cleaned

¼ cup butter, divided

1 lemon, thinly sliced

½ cup blanched slivered almonds

Preheat grill for medium heat and lightly oil the grate. Combine flour, paprika, rosemary, garlic powder, parsley, dill, salt, and pepper in a large, resealable plastic bag. Shake bag to mix contents. Place trout into bag one at a time, seal bag, and shake it to thoroughly coat trout with seasoned flour. Lay each trout onto a large piece of aluminum foil. Divide butter into four portions and add it, along with a few lemon slices and a few slivered almonds, into the cavity of each trout; press the cavities closed. Top fish with more lemon slices and almonds. Sprinkle fish with a pinch of paprika, rosemary, garlic powder, parsley, and dill. Place trout on aluminum foil sheets onto grill, and cook until fish are browned and the flesh is opaque and flakes easily, about 8 minutes per side.

KATLIN KITCHEN TROUT

2 whole (10-ounce) trout, pan-dressed

Salt to taste

Ground black pepper to taste

¼ cup all-purpose flour

4 tablespoons butter, divided

½ cup blanched slivered almonds

2 tablespoons lemon juice

1 tablespoon chopped fresh parsley, for garnish

8 slices lemon, for garnish

Rinse and pat dry trout. Season inside and out with salt and pepper to taste. Dredge trout in flour. Heat 2 tablespoons butter in a large skillet over high heat until melted. Add trout, and brown both sides. Lower heat to medium, and cook for about 5 minutes on each side or until cooked through. Transfer trout to a serving plate, and keep warm. Wipe out pan, and add 2 tablespoons butter. Cook butter over medium heat until it just begins to brown. Add the almonds, and brown. Pour sauce and almonds over fish, and sprinkle with lemon juice and parsley. Garnish with fresh lemon slices.

FISH COOKING SAFETY TIPS

When it comes to handling your catch, remember that all raw fish contain bacteria. Handle your catch as you would any perishable food by refrigerating/cooling it properly and cooking it properly too.

To ensure both quality and safety, always follow these tips:

- **Cook your fish thoroughly.** Most fish species are cooked when the meat begins to flake and the internal temperature is 145 degrees.
- **Avoid contamination.** Always keep cooked fish and raw fish away from each other. Clean and sanitize your fish workspace between cooking and serving. This includes cutting boards, counters, plates, etc.
- **Keep raw fish cold.** Keep raw fish on ice or refrigerated at 32 to 40 degrees. Thaw frozen fish in running water. I keep frozen fish packed in water until I am ready to cook.
- **Know your fish and waters.** I'm sad to say, but many of our ponds and rivers have been polluted through the years. Although programs are in place to correct this, we still must know about any pollution in our fish and waters. Check with your local fish cops (at the Department of Natural Resources) for any concerns on what you plan to catch. The same goes if you're fishing in other states or countries.

"You know you're a master fisherman when the fish just jump into your pan."

GAVIN'S MOUNTAIN TROUT

½ cup butter

3 lemons, juiced

12 fresh mushrooms, sliced

¼ cup sherry wine

3 pounds trout fillets

Salt to taste

Cracked black pepper to taste

Preheat oven to 350 degrees. Line a shallow baking dish with foil. Heat butter in a skillet over medium heat; pour in lemon juice. Cook and stir mushrooms until tender, about 5 minutes; stir in sherry. Place trout fillets with skin sides down into prepared baking dish; sprinkle with salt and cracked pepper. Pour the mushroom mixture over the fish. Bake in oven until sauce reduces and fish flakes easily with a fork, about 30 minutes.

OLLIE COBB'S BLACKENED FISH

½ cup vegetable oil

3 tablespoons fresh ground black pepper

¾ cup flour

5 pounds rainbow or brook trout fillets

(bone and skin removed)

Mix the oil and black pepper together in a mixing bowl. Coat the fish fillets with flour. Heat the skillet, then pour the oil and pepper mixture into the hot skillet. Heat the mixture until the oil starts to lightly smoke. Set the heat to low. Place the coated fillets in skillet, and cook for about 3 minutes per side, depending on size of fish.

UNCLE MARVIN'S BAKED RAINBOW

2 teaspoons olive oil (or to taste)

2 whole rainbow trout, gutted and cleaned, heads and tails still on

¼ teaspoon dried dill weed

¼ teaspoon dried thyme

Salt to taste

Freshly ground black pepper to taste

½ large onion, sliced

2 thin slices lemon (optional)

2 tablespoons hot water

Preheat oven to 400 degrees. Grease a 9- by 13-inch baking dish with about 1 teaspoon olive oil. Place trout in the prepared baking dish, and coat with remaining olive oil. Season the inside and outside of fish with dill, thyme, and salt. Stuff each fish with onion slices; grind pepper over the top. Place 1 lemon slice on each fish. Bake in oven for 10 minutes, then add water to dish. Continue baking until fish flakes easily with a fork, about 10 minutes more.

GEORGIA COOKED TROUT

Cooking spray
½ cup crushed pecans
1 teaspoon crushed dried rosemary
1 teaspoon salt

Ground black pepper to taste
All-purpose flour as needed
4 (4-ounce) trout fillets
1 egg, beaten

Preheat oven to 400 degrees. Spray a baking sheet with cooking spray. Mix pecans, rosemary, salt, and black pepper in a shallow bowl. Place flour in a separate shallow bowl. Dip trout fillets in flour, and shake off excess; dip fish into beaten egg, then into seasoned pecans, lightly pressing pecan coating onto fish. Arrange fillets on the prepared baking sheet. Bake in oven until fish flakes easily with a fork, 10 to 12 minutes.

FISH CAMP EASY GRILLED TROUT

2 whole trout, cleaned
1 tablespoon olive oil (split evenly between trout)
1 pinch coarse sea salt to taste
1 pinch ground black pepper
½ lemon, thinly sliced

½ sweet onion, thinly sliced
1 clove garlic, minced
2 sprigs fresh rosemary
2 sprigs fresh thyme

Preheat an outdoor grill for high heat, and lightly oil the grate. Rub each trout generously with olive oil, and sprinkle with sea salt; sprinkle inside of cavities with salt and black pepper. Place half the lemon and onion slices into cavity of each trout, along with minced garlic, and place a sprig of rosemary and thyme into cavities. Turn preheated grill down to low, and place the trout directly onto the grill; cook until flesh flakes easily and the skins are browned, 6 to 7 minutes per side, flipping once.

The Boys I Fish With!

Little Eddy and his mom were digging for fishing bait in the garden. Uncovering a many-legged creature, Eddy proudly dangled it before his mom.

"No, honey, that won't do for bait," she said. "It's not an earthworm."

"It's not?" Eddy's eyes went wide. "Then what planet is it from?"

CAMPFIRE TROUT

4 trout, cleaned and head removed
Salt to taste
Ground black pepper to taste

4 tablespoons butter, divided
1 medium green bell pepper, sliced
1 clove garlic, minced (optional)

Place each trout on a piece of aluminum foil. Season to taste with salt and pepper, then stuff the cavity with 1 tablespoon of butter, green pepper, and garlic if using. Roll the trout tightly in the foil, forming packets. Use some additional foil to secure each packet of fish to a metal toasting rod for use as a handle when removing fish from the coals. Cover the fish packets in the red-hot, smoldering coals of your campfire, and cook until the fish is done, 7 to 10 minutes, depending on the heat of the fire.

TROUT DIJON

Cooking spray
1 pound skinless steelhead trout fillets
¼ cup dry white wine
2½ tablespoons Dijon mustard

2 cloves garlic, pressed
1 tablespoon lemon juice
1 teaspoon dried dill weed
1 teaspoon lemon pepper seasoning

Preheat oven to 400 degrees. Spray a 9- by 13-inch baking dish with cooking spray. Arrange trout fillets in the baking dish. Mix white wine, Dijon mustard, garlic, lemon juice, dill, and lemon pepper seasoning in a bowl; spread over the fillets, letting some run underneath the fish. Bake in oven until the fish is opaque and flakes easily, 10 to 15 minutes.

BIG 10 TROUT

1 pound fresh speckled trout
2 tablespoons butter
1 tablespoon lemon pepper
1 teaspoon capers

1 pinch paprika (or to taste)
¼ cup white cooking wine
1 teaspoon minced fresh parsley (or to taste),
for garnish

Preheat oven to 400 degrees. Line a baking dish with aluminum foil. Place trout in the middle of the aluminum foil; top with butter, lemon pepper, capers, and paprika. Pour cooking wine over trout. Close foil around the trout. Bake in oven until fish flakes easily with a fork, about 30 minutes. Garnish trout with parsley.

BEER SIPPIN' TROUT

2 rainbow trout fillets	1 teaspoon ground black pepper
1 tablespoon olive oil	1 fresh jalapeño pepper, sliced
2 teaspoons garlic salt	1 lemon, sliced

Preheat oven to 400 degrees. Rinse fish, and pat dry. Rub fillets with olive oil, and season with garlic salt and black pepper. Place each fillet on a large sheet of aluminum foil. Top with jalapeño slices, and squeeze the juice from the ends of the lemons over the fish. Arrange lemon slices on top of fillets. Carefully seal all edges of the foil to form enclosed packets. Place these packets on a baking sheet. Bake in oven for 15 to 20 minutes, depending on the size of fillets. Fish is done when it flakes easily with a fork. This jalapeño flavor goes down smooth with beer!

CABIN BRAISED TROUT

1 tablespoon olive oil	4 large trout fillets
3 scallions, chopped	1 teaspoon sea salt
¼ cup dry white wine	1 teaspoon white pepper
1 tablespoon chopped fresh parsley	1 tablespoon butter

In a large black iron skillet, heat the olive oil over medium-high heat. Add the scallions and cook, stirring, until they are tender. Add the wine and parsley, and bring the mixture to a slow simmer. Add the trout fillets, season with salt and pepper, cover the skillet, and cook for about 4 to 5 minutes. Uncover the skillet, turn the trout fillets carefully, and continue cooking for about 3 more minutes. Transfer the trout to a serving platter, and cover loosely with foil to keep warm. Add butter to the skillet with the juices, and simmer until butter is melted. Serve the trout immediately, topped with sauce from the skillet. Perfect cabin vittles!

The Boys I Fish With!

A monastery was in financial trouble, so it went into the fish-and-chips business to raise money. One night, I was hungry, so I decided to check this place out.

A monk answered the door. I asked him, "Are you the Fish Friar?"

"No," he replied. "I'm the chip monk."

GREAT AMERICAN TRAILS TROUT CAKES

1 pound trout fillets, cooked and flaked

2 (5-ounce) cans tuna, drained

¾ cup bread crumbs (or more to taste)

½ cup nonfat plain yogurt

1 egg

3 tablespoons ketchup (or more to taste)

1 tablespoon dried minced onion

1 tablespoon dried dill

Cooking spray

Mix trout, tuna, bread crumbs, yogurt, egg, ketchup, onion, and dill together in a bowl. Form mixture into 6 patties. Spray an iron skillet with cooking spray, and heat over medium-high heat. Cook fish cakes in hot skillet, turning once, until cooked through and lightly browned on each side, 5 to 10 minutes. Check for seasonings, and serve.

OUTDOOR TRAILS CAMPFIRE BASS

2 cans of beer

1 shot Kentucky bourbon

1 onion, chopped

1 garlic clove, chopped

1 lemon, sliced

2 tablespoons packed brown sugar

8 medium bass fillets

In a large bowl, combine the beer, bourbon, onions, garlic, lemon, and brown sugar. Place the bass fillets in the marinade, and refrigerate for 2 hours. Place the marinated bass fillets on a roasting stick or grid, and cook over the open flames of a campfire for about 7 minutes or until the bass fillets start to flake. Season to taste, and serve hot.

EASY, TASTY BASS

1 cup peanut oil for frying (or as needed)

3 eggs

1 tablespoon water

3 striped bass fillets, skinned

1 teaspoon Cajun seasoning

1 teaspoon lemon pepper seasoning

½ cup flour

1 ounce package of salt-and-vinegar potato chips, crushed

1 lemon, cut into wedges, for garnish

Heat oil in a deep fryer or large saucepan to 350 degrees. Whisk eggs and water together in a bowl; set the egg wash aside. Sprinkle the bass fillets on both sides with Cajun seasoning and lemon pepper seasoning. Dredge the fillets in flour, and shake off any excess. Dip the fillets in the egg wash, then dip them in the crushed potato chips. Fry the fish in skillet until lightly browned, about 4 minutes per side. Serve with lemon wedges.

PHIL'S APPLE BASS

½ cup margarine, divided

4 apples, peeled, cored, and cut into thin wedges

¼ cup honey

¼ cup all-purpose flour

¼ teaspoon salt

¼ teaspoon ground black pepper

2 cups dried bread crumbs

1 egg, beaten

4 bass fillets

Melt ¼ cup of the margarine in a large skillet over medium-high heat. Fry the apples in margarine until tender. Stir in honey, reduce heat, and keep warm. In a shallow bowl, mix together flour, salt, and pepper. Place bread crumbs in another shallow bowl, and egg in a third bowl. Melt the remaining ¼ cup margarine in a large skillet over medium heat. Dredge the fish in the seasoned flour, dip in egg, then coat with bread crumbs. Place the coated fillets in the hot skillet, and cook for about 3 to 4 minutes per side. The fillets should be nicely browned, and they should flake easily with a fork. Place fish on a serving dish, and spoon the apples with honey over the top of each fillet.

HONEY BEE BASS

1 cup all-purpose flour

1 tablespoon garlic powder

1 pound bass fillets (or more to taste), cut into cubes

¼ cup Asian fish sauce

2 tablespoons olive oil

2 tablespoons honey

1 tablespoon chopped fresh oregano

2 tablespoons ouzo (anise-flavored liqueur)

Whisk flour and garlic powder together in a bowl. Toss bass in the flour mixture until coated. Whisk fish sauce, olive oil, honey, and oregano together in a bowl until smooth. Heat a skillet over medium-high heat. Cook and stir bass in the hot skillet until lightly browned on all sides, about 5 minutes. Transfer bass to a plate. Add ouzo and fish sauce mixture to hot skillet; bring to a boil. Return bass to pan, and cook until fish is cooked through, about 5 minutes more.

The Boys I Fish With!

Fish Cop: Didn't you see the "No Fishing" sign, son?

Cousin Rick: I'm not fishing, sir. I was just teaching these worms how to swim!

COUSIN RICK'S 2002 SE IOWA CHAMPION BASS VITTLES

1 cup new potatoes
1 tablespoon butter
2 portobello mushroom caps, sliced
1 red onion, sliced
1 teaspoon fresh lemon juice
Sea salt to taste

Cracked black pepper to taste
2 (4-ounce) fillets sea bass
2 tablespoons chopped fresh chervil
1 teaspoon chili oil
½ cup pesto sauce

Preheat the oven broiler. Place new potatoes in a pot with enough water to cover, and bring to a boil. Cook 10 minutes or until tender. Melt the butter in a skillet over medium heat, and sauté the mushrooms and onion until tender. Sprinkle with lemon juice, and season with sea salt and cracked black pepper. Slash the bass fillets on both sides, and insert the chervil. Rub with chili oil, sea salt, and cracked black pepper. Place fillets on a baking sheet, and broil 5 minutes on each side, or until easily flaked with a fork. Drizzle with pesto sauce, and serve over new potatoes, mushrooms, and onions. This was a great dish on a great night at an awards dinner for outdoorsmen.

SPORTSMAN BASS AND VEGGIES

5 tablespoons olive oil
1 tablespoon dried oregano
1 tablespoon dried basil
Salt to taste
Ground black pepper to taste

4 small eggplants, sliced
5 Roma tomatoes, diced
4 bass fillets
1 Roma tomato, sliced

Preheat the oven to 400 degrees. Line a baking dish with aluminum foil so that it hangs over the sides of the dish. Combine olive oil, oregano, basil, salt, and pepper in a large mixing bowl. Add eggplant and diced tomatoes, and stir to coat thoroughly with the oil mixture. Place the bass in the center of the prepared baking dish, and arrange vegetables on either side of the fish, layering sliced tomatoes on top. Raise and fold aluminum foil edges so that the fish bakes in the vegetable juice. Bake in oven until fish flakes easily with a fork and eggplant is tender, 35 to 40 minutes.

OSAGE BASS

4 small potatoes, quartered

2 tablespoons olive oil (plus more for drizzling)

2 tablespoons sherry vinegar

1 teaspoon smoked paprika (plus more for topping)

1 teaspoon kosher salt (plus more to taste)

½ cup sliced green onions

1 red jalapeño pepper, sliced

2 thick-cut boneless, skinless bass fillets

Preheat oven to 450 degrees. Oil a baking dish. Microwave potatoes on high until just softened, about 5 minutes. Whisk olive oil and sherry vinegar together in a bowl. Add smoked paprika and salt; whisk to blend. Stir in onions, jalapeño, and cooked potatoes. Slide the fish fillets into the mixture, turning and coating them with the vinaigrette. Remove the fish from potato mixture. Place potatoes in prepared baking dish. Nestle fish onto potatoes. Sprinkle with a pinch of salt, a dash of paprika, and a drizzle of olive oil. Bake in center of oven until just cooked through and fish flakes easily, about 15 minutes.

SCOUT CAMP BASS

1 lemon, juiced

3 tablespoons olive oil

2 tablespoons chopped fresh parsley

1 pinch crushed red pepper flakes

1 pinch salt

1 pound skinless bass fillets

Whisk together lemon juice, olive oil, parsley, pepper flakes, and salt in a bowl. Add bass fillets; marinate for 10 minutes in a cooler. Preheat an outdoor grill for medium-high heat, and lightly oil the grate. Grill bass until fish flakes easily with a fork, about 5 minutes each side. Discard any remaining marinade.

BAYOU BILLY'S TAVERN BASS

4 bass fillets

Salt to taste

Ground black pepper to taste

½ cup butter

3 tablespoons light olive oil

2 shallots, minced

½ teaspoon minced garlic

3 tablespoons chopped fresh parsley

3 tablespoons all-purpose flour

1 cup half-and-half

White pepper to taste

1 (16-ounce) package frozen cooked crawfish tails, thawed

1 can lump crabmeat

Preheat an oven to 350 degrees. Season the bass with salt and pepper; arrange in a baking dish, and set aside. Melt the butter with the olive oil in a skillet over medium-low heat. Cook the shallots, garlic, and parsley in the melted butter and olive oil until softened, about 5 minutes. Add the flour, and stir until completely incorporated into the mixture and the liquid is smooth. Pour the half-and-half into the mixture while stirring; cook and stir until thickened. Season with the white pepper. Gently fold the crawfish tails and crabmeat into the mixture, taking care to not break the crabmeat too much; cook another minute. Spoon the mixture over the bass fillets. Bake in oven until the fish flakes easily with a fork, 15 to 20 minutes. Serve immediately.

HAVANAN BASS

2 tablespoons extra virgin olive oil

1½ cups thinly sliced white onions

2 tablespoons minced garlic

4 cups seeded, chopped plum tomatoes

1½ cups dry white wine

²/₃ cup sliced stuffed green olives

¼ cup drained capers

¹/₈ teaspoon red pepper flakes

4 bass fillets

2 tablespoons butter

¼ cup chopped fresh cilantro

Heat oil in a large skillet over medium heat. Sauté onions until soft. Stir in garlic, and sauté about a minute. Add tomatoes, and cook until they begin to soften. Stir in wine, olives, capers, and red pepper flakes. Heat to a simmer. Place bass into sauce. Cover, and gently simmer for 10 to 12 minutes, or until fish flakes easily with a fork. Transfer fish to a serving plate, and keep warm. Increase the heat, and add butter to sauce. Simmer until the sauce thickens. Stir in cilantro. Serve sauce over fish for a great Cuban taste!

OQUAWKA FRIED CATFISH

¼ teaspoon lemon pepper
½ cup bread crumbs
¼ teaspoon garlic powder
½ cup cornmeal
⅛ teaspoon red pepper

⅛ teaspoon black pepper
¼ teaspoon sea salt
1 pound catfish fillet
1 egg with 2 teaspoons water, beaten
½ cup vegetable oil for frying

Mix together the dry ingredients, dip the fish into the egg and water mixture, and then coat the fish well with the dry mixture. Heat the vegetable oil to 360 degrees in a Dutch oven or skillet. Place the seasoned catfish in oil, cook until brown, and then turn it over and do the same. As a rule of thumb when frying catfish and other fish, cook until the fish flakes easily, about 3 to 5 minutes. With catfish and other strong-flavored river fish, I highly recommend garnishing with lemon juice and tartar sauce.

TRAIL-BLAZING CATFISH CHILI

3 tablespoons oil
1 large white onion, minced
2 garlic cloves, minced
2 tablespoons chili powder
1 teaspoon cumin
½ teaspoon coriander
1 teaspoon oregano

Cayenne to taste
1 pound canned tomatoes, drained
1 green pepper, chopped
1 (16-ounce) can kidney beans, drained
Garlic salt
Fresh ground black pepper to taste
1 pound catfish fillets, diced

In a Dutch oven over medium heat, sauté the onions, garlic, chili powder, cumin, coriander, oregano, and cayenne in the oil. Stir this mixture for a couple of minutes. Add the tomatoes, green peppers, kidney beans, garlic salt, and black pepper to taste. Stir the chili for another minute or so. Place the diced catfish fillets on top of the chili mixture, and gently stir them in. Simmer on low in the Dutch oven for about 15 minutes, and serve nice and hot. Good stuff!

FILLETING CATFISH: ANOTHER TIP FROM COUSIN RICK

Because I live in southeast Iowa, right on the Mighty Mississippi, catfish is one of the most sought-after catches. As a young angler, I learned how to clean and fillet this fish, so I want to share how to do it in a few easy steps:

1. Pat the catfish dry with a paper towel.

2. Using a sharp filleting knife, remove the dorsal and pectoral fins.

3. Fillet both sides of the fish, again making sure your knife is sharp. The skin is still on the catfish at this point.

4. Place one of the catfish fillets (skin side down) onto your cutting board. Remember to always keep your board clean and well sanitized to fight off any bacteria.

5. Make a cut through the fish meat only, not the skin. Make the cut about ¼ inch up from the tail of the fish.

6. Place the blade of your knife into the cut at a 45-degree angle, getting ready to cut against the skin, toward the head of the catfish.

7. Push the fillet knife forward, separating the skin from the meat.

8. Repeat the same steps on the other fillet, and you now have two boneless, skinless catfish fillets ready to cook and enjoy!

"I COULDN'T FIND MY POT SO I'M COOKING OUR CATCH WITH A FISH BOWL."

BLACKENED CATFISH

2 pounds smoked bacon

2 teaspoons garlic powder

2 teaspoons thyme

2 teaspoons white pepper

2 teaspoons fresh ground black pepper

2 teaspoons cayenne pepper

2 teaspoons lemon pepper

1 teaspoon allspice

1 teaspoon oregano

1 teaspoon salt

1 tablespoon olive oil

4 catfish fillets

In a Dutch oven or cast iron skillet, fry bacon; discard the bacon, and retain the bacon fat. Combine all dry ingredients, rub the catfish fillets with olive oil, and then coat the fillets with spices. Fry the catfish fillets in the hot bacon fat, and cook until you can easily flake the meat using a fork. This is a favorite dish at our fishing cabin. I love cast iron cooking!

ALEXANDRIA MO GRILLED BULLHEAD

1 tablespoon lemon juice

½ tablespoon lime juice

1 tablespoon instant coffee

½ cup salted butter, melted

½ teaspoon onion powder

½ teaspoon garlic salt with parsley flakes added

2 pounds large bullhead fillets

Combine the lemon juice, lime juice, instant coffee, melted butter, onion powder, and garlic salt in a mixing bowl, and stir well. Brush the mixture onto the bullhead fillets. Grill on medium flame for about 10 minutes per side, brushing with sauce every 5 minutes while grilling. Check for seasonings, and serve. I want to thank Jake, Skip, and Bubba J for the great times I have had fishing bullheads with them on the slough in "Alex Town": Those old boys perfected the taste of bullhead with this recipe.

SOUTHERN FRIED BLUEGILL

2 pounds bluegill fillets

1 teaspoon seasoned salt

1 teaspoon lemon pepper

2 cups dry pancake mix

Wash and pat dry the bluegill fillets, and dip into water. Sprinkle with seasoned salt and lemon pepper. Coat the bluegill lightly with pancake mix. In a skillet (I prefer cast iron), fry in deep fat for about 5 minutes. Check again for seasonings, and serve with your favorite cocktail sauce.

PICKLED BLUEGILL

½ cup vegetable oil for frying

3 pounds bluegill fillets, cut into 2- to 3-ounce portions

Salt to taste

2 large onions, peeled and sliced into rings

2 cloves garlic, chopped

8 whole black peppercorns

4 whole allspice berries

3 bay leaves

1 red chili pepper, seeded and sliced lengthwise

2 cups red wine vinegar

½ cup water

½ cup packed brown sugar (or to taste)

2 tablespoons curry powder

1 teaspoon ground turmeric

2 teaspoons ground cumin

2 teaspoons ground coriander

Heat the oil in a large skillet over medium-high heat. Season the fish with salt, and place in the skillet. Fry on both sides until fish is browned and cooked through, about 5 minutes per side. Remove from the skillet and set aside. Fry the onions and garlic in the same skillet over medium heat until translucent. Add the peppercorns, allspice berries, bay leaves, and red chili pepper. Pour in the vinegar and water, and bring to a boil. Stir in the brown sugar until dissolved. Season with curry powder, turmeric, cumin, and coriander. Taste, and adjust the sweetness if desired. Layer pieces of fish and the pickling mixture in a serving dish. Pour the liquid over until the top layer is covered. Allow it to cool, then cover and refrigerate for at least 24 hours before serving.

DONNELLSON FRIED CRAPPIE CASSEROLE

8 medium to large crappie fillets

1 cup milk

2 cups flour

1 stick salted butter

1 bell pepper, chopped

½ cup chopped onion

2 cans condensed shrimp soup

1 cup canned sliced mushrooms

4 tablespoons lemon juice

½ cup cooking sherry

1 teaspoon salt

1 teaspoon white pepper

1 tablespoon Worcestershire sauce

Soak the crappie fillets in milk for about 4 hours, then dip them in flour. In a large cast iron skillet, brown the crappie fillets in butter. Preheat oven to 350 degrees, and place the browned fillets in a baking dish. Sauté the bell pepper and onion in butter until both are tender. Add the shrimp soup, mushrooms, lemon juice, and cooking sherry, salt, pepper, and Worchestershire sauce. Simmer the sauce until bubbly. Pour the sauce over the browned crappie fillets, and bake in the preheated oven for 30 to 45 minutes.

OTTER ISLAND BEER DRINKING CRAPPIE

6 large crappie fillets

2 lemons

1 teaspoon seasoned salt

Fresh ground black pepper to taste

Garlic powder to taste

3 red potatoes

2 ears of corn, in hulls

2 tablespoons olive oil

3 tablespoons salted butter

Squeeze the juice from the lemons over the crappie fillets and season with the salt, pepper, and garlic powder. Wrap the potatoes and corn in heavy foil drenched with the olive oil. Place the crappie fillets in foil with ½ tablespoon salted butter on each, and wrap the foil tight. Place the veggies and crappie on a hot grill or fire, and cook until the crappie meat flakes and the potatoes and corn are cooked and tender. This meal goes great at camp supper while relaxing after the day's fishing trip and drinking ice-cold suds!

HERB BAKED WALLEYE

1 pound walleye

1 tablespoon butter

1 cup milk

2 tablespoons flour

½ tablespoon salt

¼ tablespoon garlic powder

1 teaspoon white pepper

½ teaspoon dried thyme

¼ teaspoon dried oregano

½ cup diced green onions

½ teaspoon paprika

Preheat oven to 350 degrees. Place the walleye in a baking dish, and dot the walleye with butter. Thoroughly blend the milk and flour. In a saucepan, cook the milk and flour over medium heat, stirring constantly until the sauce thickens and is bubbly. Stir in the salt, garlic powder, pepper, thyme, oregano, and green onions. Pour this sauce over the walleye in the baking dish, and sprinkle with the paprika. Bake the walleye uncovered for about 25 minutes or to the tenderness you desire.

RAGNAFF VIKING PICKLED HERRING

2 gallons distilled/non-chlorinated water
3¼ tablespoons seasoned salt (such as Bluing)
4 cups canning salt
1¼ cups powdered milk

2¼ tablespoons anise oil
2 garlic cloves (or more if you love garlic), minced
1 tablespoon fresh ground black pepper
About 5 dozen herring, cleaned and plug cut

In a 5-gallon bucket, add the non-chlorinated water, Bluing, canning salt, powdered milk, anise oil, minced garlic, and ground black pepper. Mix the solution well. Add up to 5 dozen herring. Cover the bucket, and refrigerate for 48 hours. Serve cold or use in your favorite recipes. Keep the bucket with fish covered and refrigerated, and it will last for weeks. This is a great and easy way to pickle herring. This brine also works well with bass, bluegill, and crappie.

DUTCH OVEN ATLANTIC COD SOUP

2 tablespoons peanut oil
1 cup sliced onion
2 cloves garlic, minced
1 teaspoon minced fresh ginger
1 large cod fillet, chopped

2 cups cooked rice
4 cups chicken broth
2 tablespoons plum sauce
2 teaspoons oyster sauce
1 large green onion, sliced

In a Dutch oven or saucepan, heat oil. Add onion and stir-fry until tender and transparent. Add garlic and ginger and stir-fry for another 30 seconds. Place the cod in the Dutch oven, reduce the heat, and cook, stirring occasionally so the cod doesn't stick to the pan. Add the rice, chicken broth, plum sauce, and oyster sauce, and bring to a boil. Cover the Dutch oven, reduce the heat, and simmer for about 10 minutes. Garnish with green onion, and serve soup with a toasted bread.

BEER DRINKING FRIED COD

1 quart oil for frying	1 pound frozen cod fillets, thawed
¾ cup all-purpose flour	2 eggs, lightly beaten
1 teaspoon salt	¾ cup crushed pretzels
½ teaspoon ground black pepper	

Heat the oil in a deep fryer to 350 degrees. Mix the flour, salt, and pepper in a large resealable plastic bag. Place cod in the bag, and gently shake to coat. Place eggs and crushed pretzels in two separate shallow dishes. Dip coated cod in the eggs, then in the crushed pretzels. Fry coated fish for 10 minutes in the preheated oil, turning once, until golden brown and easily flaked with a fork. Check for seasonings, and serve.

PORT AUGUSTA CAJUN GROUPER

¼ cup salted butter	1 teaspoon seasoned salt or sea salt (or to taste)
¼ cup flour	1 teaspoon freshly ground black pepper
1 cup chopped onion	1 teaspoon cayenne pepper
½ cup chopped celery	3 cups water
2 garlic cloves, minced	2 large grouper fillets
1 pound red tomatoes, sliced	

In a Dutch oven or cast iron skillet, cook the butter and flour together over low heat to make a roux. Add the onion, celery, and garlic, then sauté until the veggies are tender. Add the tomatoes, salt, black pepper, cayenne pepper, and water. Simmer on low heat, covered, for about 30 minutes. Add the grouper fillets, and continue cooking for 20 minutes or to your desired taste. This dish is great over wild rice.

BAYOU BILLY'S SWAMP WITCH
RED SNAPPER GUMBO

½ cup salted butter

1 cup chopped white onion

1 cup chopped celery

1 cup chopped green pepper

1 tablespoon minced garlic

1 tablespoon flour

1 teaspoon salt

1 teaspoon chili powder

1 cup diced tomatoes with juice

½ cup beer

10 ounces okra, chopped

1 pound red snapper fillets, chunked

8 ounces tomato sauce

In a large saucepan, melt the butter and sauté the onions, celery, green pepper, and garlic until tender. Combine flour with the salt and chili powder; stir into the sautéed vegetables. Add the tomatoes with their juice and beer; bring mixture to a slow simmer. Add the okra and red snapper fillets; cover and slow simmer for about 45 minutes. I serve this great-tasting fish gumbo over hot wild rice.

PENSACOLA GRILLED SHARK STEAKS

4 pounds shark steaks

5 tablespoons salted butter

2 cups chopped yellow onion

2 garlic cloves, minced

1 cup pilsner beer

½ cup cider vinegar

4 tablespoons packed brown sugar

2 teaspoons Worcestershire sauce

1 cup ketchup

Rinse the shark steaks in ice-cold water, and pat dry with paper towels. Set aside. Melt the butter in a medium saucepan. Add the onion and garlic; sauté until tender. Stir in the remaining ingredients. Bring the mixture to a boil, stirring often with a wooden spoon. Reduce the heat, and simmer for 15 to 20 minutes, or until the sauce starts to thicken. Remove from heat. Baste the shark steaks with sauce, and then place them on a well-oiled grill. Cook for 5 minutes. Baste and turn; cook another 5 minutes, or until the shark steaks flake easily with a fork.

COUSIN RICK'S HALIBUT FISH & CHIPS

3½ tablespoons cornmeal

1 cup seasoned flour

2 eggs

⅔ cup milk

¼ cup beer

Sea salt to taste

White pepper to taste

Peanut or vegetable oil for frying

4 large potatoes, peeled and sliced thin (like a chip)

1 pound halibut fillets

In a mixing bowl, combine the cornmeal, flour, eggs, milk, beer, salt, and white pepper. Mix well and set aside. In a Dutch oven or cast iron skillet, heat the oil to 350 degrees. Add the potato chips, and fry until golden brown. Place the cooked chips on a paper towel to absorb any grease. I also season the chips with salt and pepper while they're still nice and hot. Dip the halibut fillets in the batter mixture, and deep fry in oil, turning over once to ensure both sides are nice and brown. Remember, fish is done cooking when the meat flakes easily with a fork. Serve the fish and chips with tartar sauce on the side.

MRS. BECKY'S CAMPFIRE FISH WRAP

5 fresh catch-of-the-day fish (your choice)

4 tablespoons olive oil

1 teaspoon seasoned salt

White pepper to taste

1 onion, diced

3 potatoes, chopped

3 carrots, chopped

1 zucchini, chopped

Cut and scale your fish, but leave them whole. Coat the fish in olive oil, and season with salt and pepper. Place the seasoned fish with the onion, potatoes, carrots, and zucchini in heavy-duty foil, and wrap tightly. You want to have the fish steam in the foil while cooking. Place the wrapped fish on a grill or near your campfire coals. Cook the fish until the potatoes and carrots are done. This is a great recipe for teaching kids the art of outdoor cooking.

CHUCKER'S LEMON AND LIME GRILLED SALMON STEAKS

2 large fresh salmon steaks

1 lemon

1 lime

1 tablespoon extra-virgin olive oil

½ teaspoon smoked salt

½ teaspoon white pepper

1 teaspoon minced garlic

1 teaspoon cumin

3 tablespoons salted butter

Place the salmon steaks on heavy-duty aluminum foil. Grate the lemon and lime into a fine zest in a small bowl, and set aside. Squeeze both the lemon and lime over the salmon steaks, and then squeeze any remaining juice into the reserved bowl of lemon-lime zest. Season the salmon steaks with the olive oil, salt, pepper, garlic, and cumin. Slice the remaining lemon and lime, and lay over the salmon steaks. Mix the butter and lemon-lime zest, then dab a spoonful over each of the seasoned salmon steaks. Fold the foil around the salmon steaks. Place the wrapped steaks on the grill or open campfire, and cook until the meat starts to flake with a fork. Check again for seasonings, and serve.

DRY DOCK MAPLE SALMON

¼ cup maple syrup

2 tablespoons soy sauce

1 clove garlic, minced

¼ teaspoon garlic salt

$1/8$ teaspoon ground black pepper

1 pound salmon

In a small bowl, mix the maple syrup, soy sauce, garlic, garlic salt, and pepper. Place salmon in a shallow glass baking dish, and coat with the maple syrup mixture. Cover the dish, and marinate salmon in the refrigerator for 30 minutes, turning once. Preheat oven to 400 degrees. Place the baking dish in oven, and bake salmon uncovered for 20 minutes, or until easily flaked with a fork.

KICKIN' GRILLED SALMON

8 salmon fillets

½ cup peanut oil

4 tablespoons soy sauce

4 tablespoons balsamic vinegar

4 tablespoons chopped green onions

3 teaspoons brown sugar

2 cloves garlic, minced

1½ teaspoons ground ginger

2 teaspoons crushed red pepper flakes

1 teaspoon sesame oil

½ teaspoon salt

Place salmon fillets in a medium, nonporous glass dish. In a separate medium bowl, combine the peanut oil, soy sauce, vinegar, green onions, brown sugar, garlic, ginger, red pepper flakes, sesame oil, and salt. Whisk together well, and pour over the fish. Cover and marinate the fish in the refrigerator for 4 to 6 hours. Prepare an outdoor grill with coals about 5 inches from the grate, and lightly oil the grate. Grill the fillets for 10 minutes per inch of thickness, measured at the thickest part, or until fish just flakes with a fork. Turn over halfway through cooking.

CERO BLACKENED SALMON

2 tablespoons ground paprika

1 tablespoon ground cayenne pepper

1 tablespoon onion powder

2 teaspoons salt

½ teaspoon ground white pepper

½ teaspoon ground black pepper

¼ teaspoon dried thyme

¼ teaspoon dried basil

¼ teaspoon dried oregano

4 salmon fillets, skin and bones removed

½ cup unsalted butter, melted, divided

In a small bowl, mix paprika, cayenne pepper, onion powder, salt, white pepper, black pepper, thyme, basil, and oregano. Brush salmon fillets on both sides with ¼ cup butter, and sprinkle evenly with the mixture. Drizzle one side of each fillet with half the remaining butter. Cook the salmon butter side down in a large, heavy skillet over high heat until it's blackened, 2 to 5 minutes. Turn fillets, drizzle with remaining butter, and continue cooking until blackened and fish is easily flaked with a fork.

DUSTY HANSON'S GRILLED SALMON

1 teaspoon garlic powder

¼ teaspoon Accent Meat Tenderizer

¼ teaspoon seasoned salt

4 tablespoons olive oil

3 tablespoons white wine vinegar

½ cup lemon juice

2 pounds salmon steaks

Place all the marinade ingredients in a bowl, and mix well. Pour the marinade over the salmon steaks, and chill for about 3 hours or more, turning at least twice. Baste the salmon steaks while grilling with remaining marinade.

SKEETER JOHNSON'S LAZY MAN'S BBQ SALMON

1 bunch coriander, chopped

2 cloves garlic, diced

1 cup honey

1 lime, juiced

4 salmon steaks

Salt to taste

Freshly ground black pepper to taste

Oil for barbecue hot plate

In a small saucepan over medium-low heat, stir together coriander, garlic, honey, and lime juice. Heat until the honey is easily stirred, about 5 minutes. Remove from heat, and let cool slightly. Place salmon steaks in a baking dish, and season with salt and pepper. Pour marinade over salmon, then cover and refrigerate 10 minutes. Preheat barbecue for medium-high heat. Lightly oil the grill hot plate. Shake excess marinade from salmon steaks, place on grill, and cook for 5 to 8 minutes on each side, or until fish is easily flaked with a fork.

GRANDPA BLACK'S SALMON AND SMOKING BRINE

BRINE:

1 cup lemon-lime soda

1 teaspoon seasoned salt

½ teaspoon soy sauce

SALMON:

1 very large salmon fillet

Freshly ground black pepper to taste

Smoking wood plank

PASTE:

⅛ cup packed brown sugar

1 tablespoon water

Combine all brine ingredients in a large bowl or clean bucket. Soak the salmon fillet in the brine solution for at least 8 hours or overnight. Always submerge the wood plank you'll be using for smoking in water, placing a heavy object on top of it to prevent floating. Preheat an outdoor smoker for 160 to 180 degrees. Remove the salmon from the brine, rinse thoroughly under cold running water, and pat dry with paper towels. Remove the wood plank from the water and lay the fish out on the plank. Season with freshly ground black pepper. Smoke the salmon for at least 2 hours, checking after 1½ hours for doneness (although smoking a fillet can take anywhere from 2 to 6 hours depending on your taste, the size of the fillet, and the fat content of the fish). The fish is done when it flakes with a fork, but it should also not be too salty. As the fish smokes, the salt content will reduce. During the last 30 minutes of smoking, mix together the brown sugar and water to form a paste. Brush this liberally onto the salmon. Check again for taste and then EAT!

COUSIN RICK'S BBQ STEELHEAD

2 pounds steelhead trout fillets

¼ cup butter, melted

2 tablespoons lemon juice

¼ teaspoon paprika

⅛ teaspoon cayenne pepper

¼ cup barbecue sauce

Preheat an outdoor grill for medium heat, and lightly oil the grate. Arrange the trout fillets on a large piece of aluminum foil. Whisk together the butter, lemon juice, paprika, and cayenne pepper; brush the mixture onto the fillets. Cook on grill until the fish flakes easily with a fork, about 10 minutes; brush the fillets with the barbecue sauce, and cook another 2 minutes.

TASTY RIVER CARP (YES, CARP)

½ peel of small mandarin orange
3 pounds whole carp, cleaned and scaled
2 teaspoons salt
¼ cup cornstarch
2 cups sesame oil
2½ tablespoons chopped garlic
3 tablespoons minced fresh ginger root

½ cup chopped green onions
3 tablespoons dry sherry
1 tablespoon black bean sauce
2 tablespoons soy sauce
1 tablespoon sugar
6 tablespoons chicken stock

Soak the orange peel in warm water for 20 minutes or until soft. Drain, and rinse the peel under running water. Squeeze out extra liquid. Chop the peel and set aside. Make 3 or 4 slashes on either side of the fish and rub the fish with salt. Sprinkle the fish on both sides with cornstarch. Heat oil in a frying pan or wok. When the oil is hot, deep fry the fish on both sides for approximately 4 to 6 minutes per side; both sides of the fish should be browned. Remove the carp from the pan, and let it drain on paper towels. Dispose of all but 2 tablespoons of the oil (leave that oil in the pan or wok). Bring the oil back to a high heat, mix in the orange peel, garlic, ginger, and green onions. Stir fry for 30 seconds. Add sherry, bean sauce, soy sauce, sugar, and chicken stock. Mix well, then add the fish to the mixture. Cover, and let cook for 8 minutes. Serve immediately.

LAKE MICHIGAN FISH CHOWDER

2 tablespoons butter
2 cups chopped onion
4 fresh mushrooms, sliced
1 stalk celery, chopped
4 cups chicken stock
4 cups diced potatoes
2 pounds fish (use your best catch),
diced into ½-inch cubes

1 cup clam juice
½ cup all-purpose flour
⅛ teaspoon Old Bay Seasoning (or to taste)
Salt to taste
Ground black pepper to taste
2 (12-ounce) cans evaporated milk
½ cup crumbled cooked bacon (optional)

In a large stockpot, melt 2 tablespoons butter over medium heat. Sauté onions, mushrooms, and celery in butter until tender. Add chicken stock and potatoes; simmer for 10 minutes. Add fish, and simmer another 10 minutes. Mix together clam juice and flour until smooth; stir into soup, and simmer for 1 minute more. Season to taste with Old Bay Seasoning, salt, and pepper. Remove from heat, and stir in evaporated milk. Top each bowl with crumbled bacon, if desired.

FISHING BUDDIES TACOS

2 pounds tilapia fillets

2 tablespoons lime juice

2 teaspoons salt

1 teaspoon ground black pepper

1 teaspoon garlic powder

1 teaspoon paprika

Cooking spray

½ cup plain fat-free yogurt

2 tablespoons lime juice

1½ tablespoons chopped fresh cilantro

1½ teaspoons canned chipotle peppers in adobo sauce

16 (5-inch) corn tortillas

2 cups shredded cabbage

1 cup shredded Monterey Jack cheese

1 tomato, chopped

1 avocado, peeled, pitted, and sliced

½ cup salsa

2 green onions, chopped

Rub tilapia fillets with 2 tablespoons lime juice and season with salt, black pepper, garlic powder, and paprika. Spray both sides of each fillet with cooking spray. Preheat grill for medium heat and lightly oil the grate. Combine yogurt, lime juice, cilantro, and chipotle pepper in a blender; pulse until sauce is well blended. Set aside. Grill tilapia on preheated grill until fish is easily flaked with a fork, about 5 minutes on each side. Heat each corn tortilla in a skillet over medium-low heat until warm, about 1 minute. Divide grilled fish evenly over corn tortillas and serve with cilantro-lime sauce, cabbage, Monterey Jack cheese, tomato, avocado, salsa, and green onions.

SMOKEHOUSE FISH DIP

2 cups flaked smoked whitefish

2 tablespoons mayonnaise

4 tablespoons sour cream

Old Bay Seasoning to taste

Hot pepper sauce to taste

Worcestershire sauce to taste

Liquid smoke flavoring to taste

Cracked black pepper to taste

Place whitefish, mayonnaise, and sour cream in a food processor. Season with Old Bay Seasoning, hot pepper sauce, Worcestershire sauce, liquid smoke, and cracked black pepper. Blend all ingredients until consistency reaches a spread. Serve with nice salty crackers.

HOLIDAY HADDOCK

6 large haddock fillets
Salt to taste
Ground black pepper to taste
4 Roma tomatoes, thinly sliced
1 small onion, thinly sliced
1 red bell pepper, thinly sliced

1 yellow bell pepper, thinly sliced
5 tablespoons capers
8 tablespoons chopped fresh parsley
6 tablespoons extra virgin olive oil
6 tablespoons fresh lemon juice

Preheat oven to 400 degrees. Center each piece of fish on an individual piece of aluminum foil (large enough to enclose the fish when folded). Sprinkle each piece of fish with salt and pepper. Divide the sliced tomatoes, onion, and red and yellow peppers between the 6 pieces of fish, and place on top of the fillets. Sprinkle evenly with the capers and parsley. Drizzle each fillet with 1 tablespoon of olive oil and 1 tablespoon of lemon juice. Fold and seal the foil into a packet, and place on a baking sheet. Leave 2 inches between each packet for even cooking. Bake for 20 minutes. Let rest for 5 minutes, and unwrap. One packet equals one serving.

CROCKPOT HALIBUT AND SHRIMP CHOWDER VITTLES

4 slices bacon, chopped
1 onion, chopped
2 cloves garlic, minced
6 cups chicken stock
1 cup fresh corn kernels
2 large potatoes, diced
3 stalks celery, diced

2 large carrots, diced
Ground black pepper (to taste)
½ teaspoon red pepper flakes (or to taste)
1 cup scallops
1 cup uncooked medium shrimp, peeled and deveined
¼ pound halibut, cut into bite-size pieces
1 (12-ounce) can evaporated milk

Cook and stir bacon in a skillet over medium heat until browned, 5 to 8 minutes; drain excess grease. Stir onion and garlic into bacon and cook until onion is translucent, about 5 minutes. Transfer mixture to a slow cooker. Pour chicken stock into slow cooker. Mix corn, potatoes, celery, and carrots into the stock. Season with black pepper and red pepper flakes. Set the cooker to high, cover, and cook for 3 hours. Stir scallops, shrimp, and halibut into the soup, and cook 1 more hour. Stir evaporated milk into chowder, heat thoroughly, and serve.

BRADEN MANNING'S STUFFED FLOUNDER AND SEAFOOD PASTRY

STUFFING:

¼ cup butter (or margarine)

1 cup finely chopped onion

1 cup minced celery

1 tablespoon chopped fresh parsley

8 ounces crabmeat

8 ounces shrimp, peeled, deveined, and minced

¼ cup dry vermouth

Salt to taste

Ground black pepper to taste

¼ teaspoon hot pepper sauce

½ cup bread crumbs

FLOUNDER:

1 (17.5-ounce) package frozen puff pastry sheets, thawed

2 pounds flounder fillets

2 egg yolks, beaten

To make the stuffing, melt butter or margarine in a large saucepan over a medium-low heat. Sauté onion, celery, and parsley until all of the vegetables are just tender. Mix in crabmeat, shrimp, and vermouth. Season with salt, pepper, and hot pepper sauce; cook until shrimp is finished cooking (it will be pink). Mix in bread crumbs, a little at a time. When the mixture holds together well, stop adding bread crumbs. Taste, and add more seasoning (salt, pepper, and hot pepper sauce) if necessary. Set this mixture aside to let it cool. Spray a baking sheet with nonstick cooking spray. Roll a sheet of puff pastry onto a flat surface. The puff pastry, once rolled, should be about ⅓ to ¼ inch thick and large enough for you to lay the fish on top of it and still have puff pastry on the sides. Lay one of the fish fillets on top of the puff pastry. Spread the stuffing mixture evenly over the fish fillet. Place the remaining fillet over the stuffing. Trim the pastry around the fillets in roughly the shape of a fish. Save the trimmings. Roll second sheet of puff pastry out to about ⅓ to ¼ inch thick. Drape second sheet over stuffed fillets, making sure that there is enough of the top sheet to tuck under the bottom sheet of puff pastry. Trim the top sheet of pastry about ½ inch larger than the bottom sheet. Brush underside of top pastry sheet with water, and tuck under bottom sheet of puff pastry, pressing lightly to totally encase the fish and stuffing package. Place the sealed packet on the prepared baking sheet, and let it cool for 10 to 15 minutes. While packet is chilling, roll out pastry scraps. From the scraps, cut out fins, an eye, and "lips." Attach these cutouts to chilled package with a little water. Use an inverted teaspoon to make indentations in the puff pastry to resemble fish scales, but do not puncture the pastry. Chill entire package. While the package is chilling, preheat the oven to 425 degrees. Remove the fish from the refrigerator, and brush the package with the egg yolks. Measure the thickness of the package at its thickest part. Bake for 15 minutes, then reduce the temperature to 350 degrees and bake the fish for 10 extra minutes per inch of measured thickness. Test for doneness by inserting a thermometer into the package, and when the temperature reaches 140 degrees, the fish is ready to serve. You are gonna love this meal! I saved this recipe for last in this chapter because this one takes some time to prepare, but it'll be worth it when you see the smiles on the faces of the people you cooked this for.

CHAPTER 3

Small Game Cooking: Squirrel, Rabbit, Beaver, Raccoon, Muskrat, Nutria (Swamp Rat), Possum, and More

BIG HOLLOW FRIED SQUIRREL

1 cup flour
1 teaspoon seasoned salt
1 teaspoon fresh ground pepper

2 squirrels, cut into bite-size pieces
½ cup vegetable oil or shortening

Mix together the flour, salt, and pepper. In a plastic bag, shake the squirrel meat in the flour mixture to coat all sides of meat. In a Dutch oven or iron skillet, heat the oil to 350 degrees, and brown all sides of the floured squirrel meat. After all sides are browned, lower the heat, and cover the skillet. Simmer on low heat for about an hour or until meat is finished cooking. The drippings will make for a great gravy. Serve with hot buttermilk biscuits.

COUSIN RICK'S SMALL GAME TIPS

When small game carcasses arrive in the cabin kitchen, I always examine each one carefully for any shot holes if I used a shotgun as my weapon. I have found that shot holes are often marked by a nest of fur, indicating that the shot pellet has passed into the meat. Use a pair of small forceps to investigate every shot hole for any embedded pellets.

As with any game, small or large, remove any dirt and fragments of broken bone. Always trim off any meat that shows signs of bloodshot. After removing the hide, refrigerate the meat, or keep it on ice if you are at a cabin with no electricity. After making your meat cuts, freeze or prepare the game for cooking immediately. If you are like many of my hunting buddies and like to soak your game in a salt or vinegar solution, remember to do this at 40 degrees or cooler.

Recently, at a book signing, someone asked me if the age of the game affects how you should prepare it. Like most deer hunters will tell you, the old bucks are tougher than the young bucks or a doe. There are several ways to determine just how old or young an animal is, although unless you are a seasoned hunter, it can be difficult to tell. For example, the size of a rabbit can help determine age. Keen knowledge of teeth, bones, or the feather patterns on fowl will also help you figure out the age of the game.

My dad told me when I was a young gun just starting to hunt on my own that most small game are less than a year old because most small critters die in their first year. For example, did you know that 80 percent of all grouse will most likely die before reaching their first birthday?

Just be sure to follow the food safety guidelines I have recommended in this book, and you will have great tasting small game vittles!

COUSIN RICK
BOOK SIGNING

"Why yes, Mister Fudd, my book does contain quite a few recipes for wabbit stew."

TREE RAT FRICASSEE

1 young tender squirrel, cut into serving-size pieces

½ teaspoon seasoned salt

½ teaspoon fresh ground black pepper

½ cup flour (plus more if making gravy)

Vegetable oil for frying

4 to 6 slices bacon, chopped

1 tablespoon finely minced onion

2 teaspoons lemon juice

⅓ cup chicken broth

Milk for gravy (optional)

Rub the pieces of squirrel with salt and pepper, and then roll in flour. In a skillet, using very little vegetable oil, cook the seasoned meat with the chopped bacon. Pan-fry the squirrel on low for about 20 minutes, more if needed. Add the onion, lemon juice, and chicken broth, and cover the skillet. Simmer on low heat, turning every 15 to 20 minutes for about 2 hours. Just before serving, remove the squirrel meat, and you can make a great tasting gravy by adding milk and flour to the pan drippings. Mmm, mmm, good! If you like, you can double or triple this recipe—just multiply the ingredients by the number of squirrels, adjusting the seasonings as needed.

COUSIN RICK'S BRUNSWICK STEW

3 squirrels, cut into serving-size pieces

3 quarts chicken broth

½ cup diced bacon, cooked

¼ teaspoon cayenne pepper

2 teaspoons seasoned salt

¼ teaspoon fresh ground black pepper

1 cup chopped onions

4 cups stewed tomatoes, chopped

2 cups diced potatoes

2 cups lima beans

2 cups corn (I use sweet corn)

Place the squirrel meat in a Dutch oven or large kettle, and add the chicken broth. Bring the broth slowly to a boil, reduce the heat, and slow simmer for about 2 hours, skimming the surface about every 15 minutes or so. Remove the squirrel from the Dutch oven, and remove the tender meat from the bones. Return the meat to the chicken broth. Add the cooked bacon, cayenne, salt, pepper, onions, tomatoes, potatoes, and lima beans. Simmer for about an hour, then add the corn and simmer for another 30 minutes. Again, this is a great recipe for when you're out at a hunting cabin with fresh biscuits or baked bread. If you only use one squirrel recipe from this chapter, this is the one you want!

EASY BROILED SQUIRREL

1 squirrel, whole after cleaning

1 teaspoon salt

1/8 teaspoon white pepper

1/2 teaspoon fat (I prefer bacon fat)

1 lemon, sliced for squeezing juice

Take the squirrel, and rub in the salt and pepper. Brush the carcass with melted fat to coat well. Place the seasoned squirrel on broiling rack. Broil the meat for about 35 minutes, basting often with the drippings. Squeeze the juice of the lemon just before serving and recheck for seasonings.

SHIMEK FOREST BAKED SQUIRREL

1 cup flour

Salt to taste

Ground black pepper to taste

1 tablespoon Accent Meat Tenderizer

4 squirrels, cleaned and dressed for cooking

1 cup chicken broth

1/4 cup Worcestershire sauce

2 tablespoons chopped parsley

2 tablespoons minced onion

1 clove garlic, minced

1 bay leaf

Mix the flour, salt, pepper, and Accent Meat Tenderizer in a bowl. Add the seasoned flour and squirrel meat to a plastic bag, then shake until the meat is coated on all sides. Brown the meat in a roasting pan. Add the chicken broth, Worcestershire sauce, parsley, minced onions, minced garlic, and bay leaf. Bake the seasoned squirrels at 350 degrees for about 45 minutes. Reduce the heat from the oven to 220 degrees, and bake on low for another 30 minutes or until the squirrel is cooked and tender. This is also a great dish if you use a Dutch oven.

Ouch!

One time Bubba was out squirrel hunting, carrying no gun.
A game warden saw that he had several squirrels in his bag, so he asked
Bubba how he'd killed them. Bubba said, "I ugly them to death."
That game warden was amazed and asked if anybody else had ever done that.
Bubba replied, "I used to bring my wife along, but she just tore them up too badly!"

COUSIN RICK'S SQUIRREL TIPS

I believe that squirrel is one of the most tender of all wild game meats. The flesh of a young squirrel is rosy pink and truly has a great flavor. In my experience, the flesh of older squirrel is darker red in color and tougher, so I would recommend longer cooking or marinating to achieve the tender vittles that will put a smile on everyone's face.

TENDERIZING GAME MEAT

So why is older game tougher? To understand how to tenderize, you must first understand why the meat is tough to begin with. There are a few key ways in which meat becomes naturally tender, with the first being age. Simply put, age firms meat. The older the animal you're eating was, the tougher its meat will be.

Additionally, exercise can toughen meat. The more a muscle is used, the firmer and stronger it becomes. This carries over once an animal has been slaughtered, with cuts that come from areas of high activity like the legs or diaphragm being extremely tough compared to the rarely used muscles along the back.

Finally, overcooking is one way to ruin any piece of game meat no matter how tender it is normally. Cooking game meat causes the proteins to become firmer, meaning the longer a piece of meat is cooked the tougher it becomes. Longer cooking also forces moisture out of the inside of the meat, causing it to dry out if not kept moist during the cooking process. This is one of the reasons why most experienced outdoor cooks prefer rarer meat instead of well done. So, in closing, I recommend using a good brine or rub for tenderizing older game—after all, when you're beading down on Peter Rabbit with your 12-gauge, you don't have a lot of time to ask him how old he is. The trick for tougher older meat is just don't overcook it and always use a brine or marinade. Dig it? Cool!

"To make authentic Irish stew, I season it with four-leaf clovers."

©2017 Dan Roberts

MRS. MABLE'S PULASKI SQUIRREL PIE

PIE FILLING:

1 large squirrel

2 cups chicken broth

3 tablespoons flour

½ tablespoon minced parsley

1 teaspoon seasoned salt

⅛ teaspoon fresh ground black pepper

½ cup sliced mushrooms

PIE CRUST:

2 cups flour

4 teaspoons baking powder

½ teaspoon salt

¼ cup lard

⅔ cup milk

Disjoint and cut the squirrel into 2 or 3 pieces. Add enough chicken broth to barely cover the squirrel meat, and cook until tender (about 35 minutes). Take out the cooked squirrel, and remove the meat from the bones. Add the flour, parsley, salt, pepper, and mushrooms to the stock. Cook on low flame until the sauce thickens. Add the deboned squirrel meat, and stir together well. Mix the pie crust ingredients together, and roll out dough to make the crust. Add the squirrel meat mixture to the pie crust, and bake at 350 degrees, until the meat is bubbly and crust is golden brown. Mrs. Mable served this to our hunting party every deer and turkey season.

GRANDAD'S SLOW COOKED TREE RATS

2 nice-sized squirrels, cut into serving-size pieces

4 potatoes, quartered

1 pound baby carrots, chopped

1 green bell pepper, chopped

4 yellow onions, sliced

2 cups chicken broth

¼ head cabbage

1 teaspoon salt

1 teaspoon black pepper

In a slow cooker, place the squirrel meat, potatoes, carrots, green bell pepper, onions, chicken broth, cabbage, salt, and pepper. Cover, and slow cook on low for 8 to 10 hours. Serve with wild rice or fried potatoes and onions.

TAKE ME BACK TO OLD VIRGINIA
BLACK-EYED SQUIRREL

4 dressed squirrels

½ pound black-eyed peas

2 cups flour

Bacon fat for frying (plus extra lard, if needed)

3 white onions, chopped into medium slices

2 large carrots, cut into thin chunks

¾ pound smoked link sausage, cut into thin chunks

½ cup sweet peas

1 teaspoon salt (or to taste)

1 teaspoon pepper (or to taste)

1 cup chicken broth

Marinate the squirrel meat in salted water and leave in refrigerator for at least 12 hours. After soaking, rinse and pat the squirrel meat dry. In a Dutch oven or large pot, bring about 6 cups of water to a vigorous boil, and add the black-eyed peas. Boil the peas for about 5 minutes, then remove from heat and cover; hold for about 15 minutes and drain. Quarter the squirrels, and dredge in flour well seasoned with salt and pepper. Sauté the squirrel meat in bacon fat (mixed with lard if needed) until the meat is golden brown on all sides. Place the cooked meat on paper towels to absorb any extra grease. Place the cooked squirrel meat in a large crockpot.

Sauté the onions in the bacon fat and remaining pan drippings until the onions are nice and tender, then add to the cooker with meat. Add the carrots and sausage, as well as the sweet peas and reserved black-eyed peas. Season the cooker meat and veggies with the salt and pepper (more or less to your liking), and add the chicken broth. Cover the cooker and slow cook for 8 to 10 hours. My family and friends enjoy this meal when I add fried sweet potato slices on the side.

RABBIT ON THE RUN (FRIED RABBIT)

2 rabbits, cut in serving-size pieces

Flour

1 teaspoon seasoned salt

1 teaspoon fresh ground black pepper

Vegetable oil

Roll the rabbit meat in mixture of flour, seasoned salt, and pepper. Pour oil about ¼-inch deep in a large iron skillet or Dutch oven and heat it. Cooking on medium heat, place the larger pieces of rabbit first, and fry for about 15 minutes on all sides before adding the smaller pieces. Turn the rabbit pieces often for even cooking, and cook until well browned and tender (about 30 minutes). Serve with mashed potatoes and rabbit gravy made from drippings.

AMANA COLONIES HASENPFEFFER

1 rabbit, cut into serving-size pieces
1 cup Burgundy wine
6 peppercorns
3 whole cloves
1 bay leaf
1 onion, sliced
½ cup chicken broth

½ cup cider vinegar
½ teaspoon garlic salt
½ teaspoon white pepper
Flour for coating (about 1 cup)
1 tablespoon bacon fat or lard
1 cup sour cream

Place the pieces of rabbit in a crock or large glass dish. Add the wine, spices, onion, and enough chicken broth and cider vinegar in equal parts to cover the meat. Marinate the rabbit meat for at least 48 hours in the cooler or fridge. Remove the rabbit, and dry the meat well with paper towel. Sprinkle with garlic salt and pepper, and roll lightly in flour. Brown the rabbit pieces in the fat, add the marinade from meat, cover, and simmer for 1 hour on low flame. Remove the meat from the pan, and thicken the sauce/gravy while adding the sour cream. Soak the rabbit with sauce. Mmm, mmm, mmm, GOOD!

BAKED RABBIT IN THE GARDEN

2 tablespoons salted butter
1 teaspoon salt
½ teaspoon ground black pepper
1 teaspoon ground savory
1 cup chopped celery

1 cup seasoned mashed potatoes
1 large rabbit, dressed
2 large carrots, quartered
½ pound thick-cut bacon
2 cups chicken broth

Preheat oven to 400 degrees. To make the stuffing, add the butter, salt, pepper, savory, and celery to the mashed potatoes, and mix well. Fill the cavity of the rabbit with the seasoned mashed potatoes. Sew the rabbit cavity up, and place the rabbit in a deep baking pan with the legs folded under the body. Place the carrots next to the rabbit. Using toothpicks, lay the bacon over the back of the rabbit to keep the meat from drying out. Bake the rabbit for about 10 minutes, then pour in the chicken broth, and continue baking for about an hour or until the rabbit is fully cooked and the meat is tender. Just before serving, remove the bacon, and let the rabbit finish browning. Check for seasonings.

COOKING WITH RABBIT

Rabbit meat can be prepared the same as chicken. It is mild-flavored, fine-grained, and practically all white meat, so you should always cook it until it's well done, like you would chicken or turkey. As a rule of thumb, most rabbits we hunt and harvest weigh from 2 to 6 pounds, and young and tender rabbits can be cooked the same as young and tender chickens. So, on average, depending on the recipe and your cooking methods, rabbits will not require soaking in strong salt/vinegar water to remove the game taste and tenderize the meat (although you can marinate it if you like).

"YOU SAID YOU WANTED SMALL GAME, COUSIN SO I GOT MY MOUSE TRAP READY."

Lord, Save the Rabbits

The Wednesday-night service coincided with the last day of rabbit hunting season in Iowa. Our pastor asked, "Who all got their limit on rabbits this week?"

No one raised a hand. Puzzled, the pastor said, "I don't understand it. Last Sunday, many of you said you were unable to make it to service because of rabbit season. I had the whole congregation pray for your rabbits."

That's when Bubba groaned. "Well, it worked. They're all safe."

MUSTARD HARE
(RABBIT IN A MUSTARD/BRANDY SAUCE)

1 tablespoon olive oil

1 tablespoon salted butter

1 large rabbit, cut in serving-size pieces

1 teaspoon cloves

1 yellow onion, chopped

Salt to taste

Ground black pepper to taste

½ cup brandy

4 tablespoons whipping cream

2 tablespoons Dijon mustard

Heat the olive oil and butter in a large skillet. Add the rabbit meat pieces, and sauté on all sides until golden brown. While the rabbit meat is browning, add the cloves and onions. Season the meat with salt and pepper. Add the brandy slowly, and cover skillet. Simmer for about 40 minutes or until the rabbit meat is cooked thoroughly. When the meat is tender and finished cooking, remove from the skillet, and set aside. Stir in the cream and mustard, and bring to a gentle boil, stirring constantly so sauce thickens. Bring the heat back to low, add the cooked rabbit meat, coat all sides with the sauce, and serve hot.

BUCK EVE RABBIT

1 rabbit, cleaned and cut in pieces

1 teaspoon garlic salt

1 teaspoon white pepper

Flour for coating (about 1 cup)

10 thick bacon slices, cut in ½-inch pieces

1 yellow onion, chopped

8 large mushrooms, chopped

8 ounces chicken broth

1 cup sour cream

Season the rabbit meat with the garlic salt and pepper, and then dredge the seasoned meat in flour to coat well. In a heated skillet, cook the bacon until crisp. Add the rabbit meat to the skillet, and brown using bacon drippings. Add the onions and mushrooms, and sauté with the meat until tender. Preheat oven to 400 degrees. Add the chicken broth, and simmer on low for about 15 minutes, stirring sauce. Place the meat and sauce in an ovenproof dish, and bake for another 30 minutes, or until the rabbit is finished cooking. Remove the rabbit from sauce, and add the sour cream to the pan juices, stirring for about 3 minutes. Cover the rabbit with this outstanding sauce, check the seasonings, and serve. This meal is traditionally cooked the night before shotgun deer hunting opens.

BRANSON DUTCH OVEN BEAVER

1 beaver tail

3 cups dried navy beans

3 cups chicken broth

8 slices thick bacon, chopped

¼ cup molasses

3 teaspoons dry mustard

½ cup minced white onion

1 garlic clove, minced

2 teaspoons smoked salt

1 cup beer

Carefully and safely skin the beaver tail by using a gas torch, charring until the skin starts to blister and separate. Take the meat from the tail, and cube it. Place the navy beans in a Dutch oven, cover with chicken broth, and bring to a boil. Boil the beans for about 10 minutes. After cooking, remove the navy beans and broth, and let stand for about an hour. Add the chopped bacon and beaver meat to the Dutch oven, and cook until bacon is crisp. Add the reserved beans and chicken broth. Add the remaining ingredients, and cover the Dutch oven. Bring the mixture to a slow boil, reduce the heat, and simmer on low for about 8 hours, adding more beer and broth if needed. Check for seasonings, and serve.

CROTON CREEK ROAST (BEAVER TAIL)

1 beaver tail

1 bottle of red wine

½ cup cider vinegar

1 teaspoon garlic salt

Flour, seasoned with salt and pepper

1 egg

Olive oil

Seasoned bread crumbs

3 tablespoons salted butter, melted

Marinate the beaver tail in the red wine for at least 24 hours, and then pat dry. Simmer covered in water with the vinegar and salt until the beaver meat is close to being thoroughly cooked. Preheat oven to 375 degrees. Remove the tail, and pat dry again. Dust the tail with seasoned flour, then dip in egg beaten with a little olive oil, then into the seasoned bread crumbs. Place the seasoned beaver meat onto a greased rack, coat with butter, and roast in oven until the meat is brown and tender. This beaver tastes great, and will be a big hit at any wild game feast.

COOKING WITH BEAVER

Beaver is a true fur-bearing animal; prime beaver pelts always bring in a good price on the market. Beaver meat is dark, rich, and truly tasty, but always keep in mind that beaver has the possibility of carrying tularemia (which is noticeable when skinning). Beaver also have glands that you will need to remove while skinning: a castor gland near the tail under the belly and musk glands in the small of the back under the forelegs. Try not to damage these glands while removing them.

As with most game, remove the surface fat, and hang the carcass in a cool area for a couple of days. I highly recommend marinating large beaver in a plastic bucket using water to cover the animal with 1 tablespoon vinegar and 1 tablespoon salt per gallon of water. Another good trick is adding onion juice to the marinade.

COOKING WITH RACCOON

Raccoons should have all the fat, inside and out, removed, and like the beaver, you should remove all the glands that are under the legs, along the spine, and under the small of the back. Raccoon meat is very dark and long fibered, with a course texture. When cooking with "coon," I highly recommend parboiling before starting the cooking process. The brine solution that I suggested in the beaver recipe on page 51 will work just fine for coon.

Hunting For Nuts

I remember when Bubba took me hunting for the first time. He kept reminding me to stand still and be quiet.

An hour into the woods, Bubba heard me screaming behind him.

"I thought I told you to be quiet!" said Bubba.

"Hey, I kept quiet when the snake bit me," I said. "And I was quiet when the fox attacked me. But then these two little tree rats crawled up my pant leg, and I swear I heard one ask the other, 'Should we eat them now or take them with us?'"

LAKE WYAKINS BEAVER IN SOUR CREAM

1 beaver, skinned and cleaned
½ cup cider vinegar
1 tablespoon salt
2 quarts water
2 teaspoons baking soda

½ cup flour
½ teaspoon paprika
¼ cup salted butter
1 large onion, sliced
1 cup sour cream

Soak the beaver for 24 hours in a solution of ½ cup cider vinegar and 1 tablespoon salt added to enough cold water to cover. Remove the beaver from the brine, and wash and cover with a solution of the baking soda and water. Bring to a boil, reduce heat, and simmer for about 15 minutes. Meanwhile, preheat oven to 350 degrees. Drain and rinse the beaver and cut into serving-size pieces. Dredge each piece of meat thoroughly in the flour seasoned with the paprika. Melt the butter in an iron skillet or heavy frying pan, and brown the seasoned meat. Transfer the meat to a well-greased casserole dish, and add the sliced onion on top. Add 2 cups water, and bake until tender. Five minutes before the meat is done, add the sour cream, stir well, and finish the bake. Check for seasonings, and enjoy!

COON IN BBQ

1 cleaned raccoon, cut into serving-size pieces
1 cup red wine
2 onions, sliced
3 bay leaves
1 tablespoon salt

1 teaspoon white pepper
3 garlic cloves, sliced
2 cups barbecue sauce
1 tablespoon paprika

Place the coon pieces in a large pan. Add the wine, onions, bay leaves, salt, pepper, and garlic. Bring to a boil. Cover and simmer on low for about an hour. Remove the meat and drain. Preheat oven to 350 degrees. Place the coon in a greased baking dish. Mix the barbecue sauce and paprika together, and pour over coon meat. Bake for about 70 minutes, check for seasonings, and serve.

RICK ROE ROASTED COON AND YAMS

1 raccoon, dressed	4 large yams, peeled and cut in quarters
2 red pepper rods	1 cup water
Lemon juice	¼ cup packed brown sugar
1 teaspoon salt	½ teaspoon cinnamon
¼ teaspoon white pepper	½ teaspoon ginger
⅛ teaspoon sage	

Place the coon in a large pot with the peppers. Cover with water, and bring to a boil. Remove the coon from the pot, and place on a rack in a roasting pan. Preheat oven to 350 degrees. Pour lemon juice on the coon. Sprinkle with salt, pepper, and sage. Place the yams in the pan around the coon meat. Add the water. Mix together the brown sugar, cinnamon, and ginger, and sprinkle on the yams. Cover and bake for about 2 hours, or until the meat is golden brown and tender. Check again for seasonings, and serve. This recipe is a hunting camp favorite!

COUSIN RICK'S ROASTED COON

1 large yellow onion, chopped	1 teaspoon marjoram
1 cup celery, chopped	½ teaspoon mace
4 tablespoons butter	¼ cup orange juice
½ pound deer sausage (or ground sausage meat)	2 teaspoons salt
¼ cup cream	1 teaspoon fresh ground pepper
2 cups corn bread crumbs	1 large raccoon, dressed but not cut into serving size
2 teaspoons sage	1 cup red wine
3 tablespoons chopped parsley	

In a large cast-iron skillet, sauté the onions and celery in the butter. Add the deer sausage and cook until brown. Drain off any fat. Preheat oven to 310 degrees. In a large bowl mix, together the sausage mixture, cream, corn bread crumbs, sage, parsley, marjoram, mace, and orange juice thoroughly. Salt and pepper the coon inside and out. Stuff the raccoon and close up the belly cavity. Place on a rack in a roasting pan, add the wine, and bake for about an hour per pound of meat. Turn the coon meat over at the halfway time to ensure all sides are baked. Baste with the drippings frequently during the baking time. Check for seasonings, and serve hot.

MAY RANCH RACCOON STEW

1 raccoon, cut into bite-sized cubes

Vegetable or olive oil (optional)

3 onions, sliced

3 cups canned tomatoes, chopped

1 teaspoon salt

1 teaspoon fresh ground black pepper

1 bay leaf

1 tablespoon Worcestershire sauce

1 cup chopped carrots

1 cup chopped potatoes

1 cup chopped turnips

Brown the coon meat cubes slowly in a Dutch oven. If needed, add vegetable or olive oil. Add the onions during the last of the browning process so they do not scorch or burn. Reduce the heat, and add enough tomatoes and water to cover the coon meat. Season with salt, pepper, bay leaf, and Worcestershire sauce, and then cover. Simmer on low heat until tender. Add the chopped veggies, and continue to simmer until the veggies are tender. Check for seasonings, and serve with hot buttermilk biscuits.

TENDER COON MADE EASY

1 raccoon

2 tablespoons salt

1 teaspoon black pepper

1 cup flour

¼ cup salted butter

2 cups beef broth

Clean the raccoon, and remove all the fat. Cut into 8 to 10 pieces, rub meat with salt and pepper, and roll in flour. Cook in hot butter until the coon meat is good and brown, add the beef broth, cover, and simmer on low heat for about 3 hours. Check for seasonings, and serve.

TODD LARSON'S HUNTING BUDDIES CROCKPOT COON VITTLES

1 nice-sized raccoon

¼ cup honey

1 cup chicken stock

3 tablespoons cider vinegar

3 tablespoons cream sherry

2 tablespoons soy sauce

½ teaspoon garlic salt

Clean the raccoon, quarter, and remove any surface fat. Put the pieces into a large crockpot. Mix all the remaining ingredients, and pour over meat pieces. Cover, and slow cook for at least 8 hours. Remove meat and discard the fat before thickening the remaining liquid for the gravy. This meat will come out brown, tender, and very tasty.

CARROT-STUFFED MUSKRAT

SALTED WATER SOLUTION:

1 quart water

2 tablespoons salt

STUFFED MUSKRAT:

1 medium to large muskrat

4 large potatoes

3 tablespoons salted butter

Seasoned salt, to taste

1 teaspoons fresh ground pepper

1 teaspoon savory

1 cup chopped celery

2 large carrots, quartered

6 thick slices of smoked bacon

2 cups hot water

Clean and soak the muskrat overnight in salted water (2 tablespoons salt to 1 quart of water). Cook the potatoes, and mash with the butter, then season with seasoned salt, pepper, savory, and celery. Preheat oven to 400 degrees. Fill the muskrat with the potato stuffing, and sew up. Rub the muskrat on all sides with seasoned salt. Place in a roasting pan with the legs tied under the body. Place carrots on the rack beside the meat. Lay the bacon strips on the back of the meat. Bake for 20 minutes, then pour 2 cups of hot water over the body, and continue baking for about 75 more minutes. For the last 15 of those minutes, remove the bacon to brown the back of the meat.

MUSKRAT MEATLOAF

SALTED WATER SOLUTION:

1 quart water

2 tablespoons salt

MEATLOAF:

3 pounds muskrat meat

½ teaspoon thyme

1 teaspoon garlic salt

2 eggs, beaten

1 teaspoon Worcestershire sauce

1 cup dry bread crumbs

Salt to taste

1 teaspoon ground black pepper

1 cup evaporated milk

1 white onion, grated

Mix the salt with the water, and soak the muskrat overnight. Drain the water, remove the meat from the bones, and grind the meat. Preheat oven to 350 degrees. After grinding, mix the meat with the remaining ingredients. Place the seasoned ground muskrat in a meatloaf dish. Bake for about 2 hours, and check for seasonings before serving. When it's done, there should be no pink in the loaf.

COOKING WITH MUSKRAT

The muskrat is a true furbearer, also known in fancy restaurants and in some areas as the "marsh rabbit" (although there is another creature also called the swamp or marsh rabbit). It is noted for its clean eating habits: It's a vegetarian and, as such, seldom eats anything to give its dark meat an "off" flavor. Just like the beaver, muskrat can carry tularemia. Like the beaver and most other small game, the fat has a very strong taste, so I highly recommend removing it all before cooking. Also like the beaver, these little critters have glands that need to be removed.

Rookies!

One day, when Bubba and I were still new deer hunters, we decided to separate to increases our chances.

"Hey, what if we get lost?" said Bubba.

I thought about this a bit. "Fire three shots up in the air, every hour on the hour," I said. "I saw it on TV."

Sure enough, Bubba got himself lost, so he fired three shots up into the air every hour on the hour.

The next day I finally managed to find Bubba with the help of a forest ranger.

"Did you do what I said?" I asked.

"Yes," said Bubba. "I fired three shots up into the air, every hour on the hour, right up until I ran out of arrows."

COOKING WITH OPOSSUM (POSSUM)

The possum is a chubby little critter with a very distinctive flavor of meat. My grandfather always told me that possum should be dressed just like a suckling pig, by removing the entrails as well as the head and tail. Like other small game, soaking overnight with a salt water solution helps with the cleaning of the animal. For possum, I cover the carcass with ice-cold water mixed with 1 cup salt. Half a cup of cider vinegar in the solution also helps with the flavor.

GAVIN WILLIAMS'S MUSKRAT AND ONIONS

SALTED WATER SOLUTION:

1 quart water

1 tablespoon salt

MUSKRAT AND ONIONS:

1 large muskrat, dressed and disjointed

2 teaspoons seasoned salt

1 teaspoon paprika

½ cup flour

4 tablespoons salted butter

3 onions

Garlic salt (optional)

1 cup sour cream

Soak the muskrat overnight in salted water solution. Season with seasoned salt and paprika, roll the meat in flour, and fry in a skillet with butter until meat is nice and brown on all sides. Cover the meat with the onions (garlic salt is a great seasoning to use here). Add the sour cream, cover skillet, and allow to simmer on low for about 1 hour. Check again for seasonings, and serve hot. This recipe is dedicated to Gavin, aka "The GW," his grandpa's pride and joy!

LOUISIANA SWAMP RAT

2 large nutrias

Chicken broth

1 quart water

2 teaspoons salt

2 teaspoons fresh ground pepper

2 onions, sliced

1 cup butter

2 cups ketchup

2 teaspoons Worcestershire sauce

Cayenne pepper to taste

Soak the nutria overnight in salted chicken broth. Drain, disjoint, and cut into serving-size pieces. Place in a deep pan, and add water, salt, pepper, and onions. Bring the mixture to a boil, and then simmer on low for about 1 hour. In a large cast-iron skillet, fry the nutria pieces in butter until golden brown. Add the remaining ingredients, including cayenne pepper to taste, and simmer on low heat until a thick gravy forms. Check again for seasonings, and serve with fried cornbread. Mmm, mmm, good! This is a holiday favorite for the great folks that hunt and fish the swamplands. I want to thank my fishing friend Timmy (Bubba T) and his beautiful wife Bella for sharing this fried nutria recipe with me.

JIM O'NEAL'S MICHIGAN POSSUM STEW

1 large possum, cut into serving-size pieces
½ cup oil
2 garlic cloves, minced
1 onion, sliced
6 carrots, chopped

8 ounces tomato juice
1 teaspoon Tabasco
1 teaspoon salt
1 teaspoon black pepper
6 potatoes, peeled and sliced

Brown the possum meat in oil in a Dutch oven. Add all ingredients except the potatoes. Cover and simmer on low for about an hour. Add the potatoes and simmer for another 40 minutes, then check for seasonings and serve.

POSSUM & GRAVY

1 possum, cut in serving-size pieces
Butter or lard (for frying)
2 cups chicken broth
1 can cream of mushroom soup
Flour (about 1 cup)
Water (just enough to thicken gravy)

1 large yellow onion, chopped and sautéed
½ cup wine (I use homemade red wine)
½ teaspoon oregano
½ teaspoon rosemary
1 teaspoon seasoned salt
1 teaspoon fresh ground black pepper

Fry the possum in fat such as butter or lard in a large pan. Add the chicken broth and mushroom soup, and stir up the pan to get the brown bits. Thicken the gravy with flour and water. Mix in the remaining ingredients, stir well, and simmer on low heat, stirring frequently, for about 45 minutes. Serve meat with gravy over hot buttermilk biscuits.

YARLEM CAMP POSSUM STEW

1 possum, cut up into chunks
2 cups seasoned flour (salt and pepper)
Cooking oil
1 cup chopped onions
1 can hot chili peppers

1 teaspoon black pepper
1 cup red wine
1 (10-ounce) can tomato sauce
1 (10-ounce) can beef broth

Dredge the possum chunks in seasoned flour to coat well. Brown the seasoned chunks in a hot skillet with cooking oil. Add the remaining ingredients. Stir, and cover the skillet. Reduce the heat, and simmer on low for about 1½ hours, stirring occasionally. Check stew for seasonings, and serve with cornbread.

BEANS AND POSSUM VITTLES

1½ cups navy beans
1 cup cooked and diced possum meat
2 cups diced ham
1 teaspoon garlic salt

1 teaspoon white pepper
1 cup chopped onions, for garnish
Parsley, for garnish

Wash and rinse the navy beans in cold water at least twice. In a heavy pan or Dutch oven, cover the beans in cold water. Bring the beans to a boil, and continue boiling for about 20 minutes. Pour off the water, and rinse again. After rinsing, add enough fresh water to the beans to cover them about 2 inches. Add the diced possum meat and diced ham meat. Cook on low heat for about 3 hours, stirring occasionally, and add more water if needed. Add the garlic salt and white pepper, and adjust to taste. Serve with fried potatoes, and garnish with chopped raw onions and parsley.

OLD HICK POSSUM MEAT POT PIE

1 large pie crust
1 medium possum, cooked and diced
1 cup glazed huckleberries

½ cup thin-sliced carrots
½ cup sliced red cabbage
3 ounces dry gin

Preheat oven to 350 degrees. Cover a baking pie pan with the pie crust, and place the cooked, diced possum meat in the bottom of the crust. Add the huckleberries and carrots; sprinkle all with the red cabbage. Add your favorite seasonings. Close up the pie crust, and bake for about 1½ hours. Remove the possum meat pie, slice it, and enjoy!

CHAPTER 4

Big Game Cooking: Bear, Buffalo, Wild Boar, Moose, Caribou, Elk, Whitetail, and Antelope

B ig game hunting is truly a dream come true for an average guy like me. But there are several things that you and your hunting party need to know before you go afield to bag your game, so I wanted to share a few tips that will help.

Be Prepared

The first thing to remember is don't let your enthusiasm for the hunt interfere with your preparations for handling game in the field. You should be prepared for the kill. Be sure to make a list of items you'll need to help take home your harvest. What you use will depend on the big game you're seeking, but I have listed just a few of the basics:

- 12 feet of quarter-inch rope to drag the game.
- A very sharp hunting knife (4- to 6-inch blade) to field dress.
- A yard of string to tag the game and tie the bung.
- A plastic bag to hold the heart and liver.
- At least 4 pairs of latex gloves for your hands while field dressing.
- Several clean towels or cloths to clean out the excess blood or intestinal contents of the animal's body cavity and to dry your wet hands.

Safety First

Always strive for a quick, clean kill. Make sure you have a good shot before pulling the trigger, then be sure your game is dead. Never walk up to the animal immediately after the shot. Many hunters have been caught off guard when an animal they thought was dead suddenly jumped up and charged them or ran off. I always get into a safe position to observe the downed beast and will try to wait 15 to 20 minutes before approaching. That way, if the animal gets up, I will be able to shoot it again if needed. Even if you knock the game down and it gets up and runs out of sight, wait at least 20 minutes, unless it's raining or snowing heavily. If the animal is mortally wounded, it will most likely stop, bleed, lie down, and die. Note the shape of each blood droplet to determine the direction of travel.

Tagging the Game

According to most states' Fish and Game regulations, the first step is to tag your game. This information helps states manage big game by supplying information on the location and number of game. While the old advice was to bleed your animal by sticking or cutting the throat, this is not recommended unless the animal is shot in the head or the backbone is broken. Most modern firearms ordinarily take care of the bleeding without additional cutting. Do NOT cut the throat if you plan to mount the head. If you think the animal needs additional bleeding, field dress it, then cut the main artery next to the backbone.

Field Dressing Big Game

Always use care when field dressing your game. Contaminating the carcass with intestinal contents, getting hair all over the meat, and getting dirt, leaves, and trash in the body cavity are some of the most common errors big game hunters make. Keep the carcass as clean as possible, and follow these steps to produce the delicious big game meat you worked so hard on. After all, my cool recipes won't be any use if your meat is not processed correctly.

If possible, drag the animal to a spot where you will have plenty of room to work. Try and prop it on its back with a rock or a tree limb. Cut around the anus, then draw it out, and tie it off with a string. Be sure to cut it free so that it will pull out with the intestines. Also, be sure at all times to cut from the inside of the hide to prevent loose hair from getting onto the meat. To make the first cut, lift the hide between the legs, insert the point of the knife, and make a small opening. Then insert two fingers of your free hand into the opening, and lift the hide. Carefully cut the hide from the inside along the midline of the belly to the breastbone. Roll the carcass onto its side. Draw the anus through the pelvic opening, and roll the intestines out onto the ground. Cut the esophagus just forward of the paunch, and remove the remaining viscera. Carefully lift the bladder, cut the ligaments around it, and remove it. Some of my hunting buddies prefer not to cut the pelvic bone, remove the pluck, or split the chest cavity until the game is butchered or at least until they get back home or to camp where they can use a saw or hatchet. This helps keep flies and yellow jackets, as well as contamination, out of the body cavity by minimizing the opening—especially if you have to drag the animal a long distance.

Once the abdominal cavity is open, cut the diaphragm away from the ribs. Reach in, and cut the windpipe and esophagus forward of the lungs. Remove the heart, lungs, and esophagus. With really big game like moose or bear, you will most likely need help with this. Next cut loose the liver and heart, and put them in plastic bags for transporting. Some big game such as deer does not have a gall bladder, so you can handle the liver without fear of rupture and contamination.

Tilt the carcass over, and drain out any free blood or blood clots, then thoroughly wipe out the body cavity with a clean, dry cloth. If the animal is gut shot, do some trimming to remove any contamination on the meat. These steps are important, since a lot of unwanted "gamey" taste in large game comes from flavors absorbed from the spilled intestinal contents. Do not use stream water to wash out the body cavity, as keeping the surfaces dry will reduce spoilage.

If you have performed all these steps correctly, your big game should be ready to drag back to camp or truck. (Unless you are one of those rich dudes who have it done for you.) If you want the head for a trophy, be careful as you drag your game out. I learned the hard way that a long drag will wear off the hair.

Again, refrigerate the carcass as soon as possible for the best quality of meat, ideally within 3 to 5 hours after killing if the temperature is above 50 degrees. The best device I have found for hanging the carcass with the head down is a large gambrel, a very strong rod or stick notched at both ends and the middle.

Skin the hind legs from just below the hock to about 4 inches above the hock. Place the notched stick between the tendon and leg, and spread the legs apart. Tie a rope to the center of the stick, and hang the carcass. After the animal is hung, the remaining dressing steps can easily be accomplished.

MADISON FARMS GARLIC BEAR

8 pounds bear meat, trimmed of fat and soaked in soy sauce for 24 hours

8 tablespoons salted butter

6 tablespoons fresh ground black peppercorn

4 tablespoons garlic salt

3 ounces Kentucky bourbon

After the bear meat has been soaked in the icebox, covered with the soy sauce, put it in a large Dutch oven, and brown the meat in butter. Add the remaining ingredients, and cook until all the liquids have boiled. Reduce the heat in the Dutch oven, and simmer on low for 30 minutes. Check for seasonings, and serve with warm garlic rolls or bread.

COUSIN RICK'S
BIG GAME HUNTING CHECKLIST

I cannot count how many times my hunting buddies and I have arrived at camp, only to realize we've forgotten critical hunting gear! To spare you this same misery, the following is a checklist that can help you remember all the most important things to bring for your next trip:

For Your Day Hunt Pack

- ❏ Big game license
- ❏ Hunter safety card (if required by the state)
- ❏ Weapon (with ammo)
- ❏ Bore sight
- ❏ Hunting gloves, both light and heavy camo
- ❏ Waterproof matches
- ❏ Toilet paper
- ❏ Sharp 4-inch knife
- ❏ Knife sharpener
- ❏ 25 feet of rope
- ❏ Compass
- ❏ Map (if you're hunting without a guide)
- ❏ Water

- ❏ Food/protein snack
- ❏ Any medications you'll need
- ❏ Flashlight and batteries
- ❏ Emergency blanket
- ❏ Cell phone or GPS, with charger
- ❏ Rangefinder
- ❏ Two-way radio
- ❏ Game bags
- ❏ Hand warmers
- ❏ Rubber or latex field-dressing gloves
- ❏ Game calls
- ❏ First-aid kit
- ❏ Extra batteries

Recommended Cooking Supplies

- ❏ Coffee
- ❏ Coffee pot
- ❏ Dry, smoked, or canned foods
- ❏ Ketchup/mustard
- ❏ Salt and pepper
- ❏ Spices
- ❏ Butter or cooking oil
- ❏ Forks, knives, spoons
- ❏ Plates
- ❏ Bowls
- ❏ Spatula

- ❏ Tongs
- ❏ Can opener
- ❏ Aluminum foil
- ❏ Paper towels
- ❏ Dutch oven and tripod
- ❏ Cast iron skillet
- ❏ Pots and pans
- ❏ Griddle
- ❏ Zippered plastic bags
- ❏ Propane stove
- ❏ Lighter

Camp Site

- [ ] Tent, frame, and spikes (if not at a cabin)
- [ ] Wood stove
- [ ] Propane or lantern fuel
- [ ] First-aid kit
- [ ] Duct tape
- [ ] Table
- [ ] Folding chairs
- [ ] Lanterns
- [ ] Cot
- [ ] Sleeping bag
- [ ] Waterproof tarps
- [ ] Axe
- [ ] Hammer
- [ ] Shovel
- [ ] Game hoist
- [ ] Dish soap
- [ ] Trash bags
- [ ] Coolers
- [ ] Water containers
- [ ] Toilet paper

Vehicle

- [ ] Extra gas
- [ ] Tools
- [ ] Tow chain
- [ ] Jack
- [ ] Bungee cords
- [ ] Cell phone/GPS

Personal Care

- [ ] Toothbrush and toothpaste
- [ ] Soap
- [ ] Prescription and over-the-counter medications

Hunting Gear

- [ ] Your bow, rifle, muzzleloader, etc.
- [ ] Extra bullets or broadheads
- [ ] Gun or bow case
- [ ] Gun cleaning kit, with oil and wipes
- [ ] Scope covers
- [ ] Gut knife
- [ ] Game bags
- [ ] Binoculars
- [ ] Game saw
- [ ] Extra batteries
- [ ] Flashlight
- [ ] Cell phone or GPS, with charger
- [ ] Camera

Clothing

- [ ] Heavy coat (or insulated bib/coveralls)
- [ ] Light coat (or light insulated bib/coveralls)
- [ ] Solid fluorescent orange coat/vest/head cover
- [ ] Gloves
- [ ] Ball cap or stocking cap (or at least ear muffs)
- [ ] Sunglasses
- [ ] Sweatshirts
- [ ] Insulated shirts
- [ ] Insulated pants
- [ ] Socks
- [ ] Boots (both heavy insulated and lightweight hiking)
- [ ] Long johns
- [ ] Gun belt
- [ ] Shoes
- [ ] Rain gear
- [ ] Extra boot laces

GRANDMA BLACK'S MICHIGAN MEATLOAF

3 pounds ground bear meat	2 cups seasoned bread crumbs
32 ounces French onion soup	½ cup ketchup
3 eggs	1 tablespoon garlic powder
12 mushrooms, chopped	1 tablespoon fresh ground black pepper

Preheat oven to 360 degrees. Add all the ingredients together in a large mixing bowl, and mix well. Let the mixture stand for 20 minutes. Form the mixture into a loaf. Bake the loaf for approximately 2½ hours or until no longer pink in center. Serve with fried potatoes and gravy.

COUSIN RICK'S BEAR CAMP STEW

6 pounds bear meat, cubed	6 cups beef stock/broth
6 tablespoons salted butter	1 tablespoon dried bay leaves
2 tablespoons olive oil	10 small red potatoes
1 cup all-purpose flour	4 carrots, peeled and diced
2 tablespoons seasoned salt	2 turnips, cubed
2 yellow onions, sliced	

Preheat a Dutch oven on medium flame. Brown the bear meat in butter and olive oil. Blend all the remaining ingredients together in a large mixing bowl. Check for seasonings, and add to the preheated Dutch oven. Cook on medium/low heat for about 3 hours, basting and stirring often until veggies are tender. If needed, add beer or more stock.

OLD HUNTER BEAR MUSH

10 pounds bear roast or meat, cubed	Salt to taste (plus more if you plan to cure the meat)
4 pounds white onion	Ground black pepper to taste
1 pound navy beans, cooked	5 cups beer
Bacon fat	

In a large Dutch oven over a campfire, cook all ingredients in order. Bring to a boil, and then reduce heat and simmer for about an hour or until beans are tender. If you plan on using this as camp food for hunting trips, add ½ cup of salt with the leftovers, depending on weather and hunting conditions, as a cure.

COOKING WITH BEAR

When cleaning bear, remove all possible fat. Also keep the carcass as cool as possible, since bear has a large amount of fat, and fat becomes rancid much faster than meat.

Although other states have bear, the following are my favorites for hunting (I rank Idaho and northern Wisconsin as tied for best black bear hunting).

Best States to Hunt Wild Bear

- Alaska
- North Carolina
- Arizona
- Northern Wisconsin
- Idaho

TREE STAND SAFETY HARNESS

Nothing gets you kicked out of my hunting group quicker than refusing to wear a safety harness when you're hunting from a tree stand. The usual excuse is, "It won't happen to me." The average age of victims who fell or hung to their death in tree-stand hunting accidents is 44 years. These were tree-stand hunters with 20 years of experience who got lazy and too familiar with the risks. In 75 percent of the deaths, the subject was not wearing a full-body harness. In this group, 55 percent were using climbing stands and 45 percent lock-on or ladder stands. Most tree-stand accidents occur when the hunter is getting into or out of the stand or when putting up or taking down a tree stand. For the most part, hunters believe it can't happen to them. Many believe that if they do lose their balance, they will quickly grab something to stop their fall and regain their balance. Both of these assumptions are wrong. While lock-on and ladder stand accidents are common, climbing accounts for a lot of accidents, too, mostly when a hunter fails to attach the top and bottom sections of the stand and then loses the foot climber. Another sure way to get into trouble is to attempt to level a stand while sitting in it. I call not wearing a safety harness in a tree stand a dumb attack!

You Gotta Believe

A bear hunter who was an atheist was out in the woods when suddenly a 1,000-pound black bear stepped out.

"Good God!" said the hunter.

Suddenly, a voice from Heaven said, "I thought you don't believe in me."

The hunter replied, "Yeah, well up until now, I didn't believe in 1,000-pound black bears either."

BOW KILL BEAR MEAT

2 pounds bear steaks

1 quart tomato juice

¾ cup brown sugar

4 tablespoons Worcestershire sauce

1 tablespoon fresh ground black pepper

1 tablespoon celery seed

1 white onion, diced

1 tablespoon cayenne pepper

In a slow cooker, cook the bear meat for about 3 hours on medium. Drain the fat from the cooker, and add all the remaining ingredients. Simmer on low heat for another 90 minutes. Check for seasonings, and serve the gravy with mashed or fried potatoes.

MAJOR BLACK'S WINTER OF 1881 WAR MEAT CHILI

½ cup olive oil

1 pound ground bear meat

1 pound bear steak, cubed

3 cups chopped onions

1 cup chopped green peppers

¼ cup chopped celery

5 garlic cloves, minced

4 jalapeño peppers, seeded and chopped

½ cup corn flour

$1/3$ cup chili powder

1 tablespoon ground cumin

1 teaspoon white pepper

1 tablespoon salt

20 ounces tomatoes

In a Dutch oven or large pot, brown all the meat in oil, and then drain the fats and drippings. Add the remaining ingredients, and simmer on low flame for about 3 hours. Season to taste, and serve with cornbread or toast. This recipe was passed down word for word by my grandpa, who got it from his father. I'm told that even though my great-grandpa Black was a major in the Civil War with his own mess cooking team, he preferred to cook this meal on his own.

RODEO BISON STEAKS

6 medium-size buffalo steaks

Buttermilk

Flour

½ stick salted butter

1 tablespoon garlic powder with parsley

½ tablespoon seasoned salt

½ tablespoon fresh ground black peppercorn

1 cup sliced mushrooms (morels if in season)

1 cup beer

In a large glass dish, cover the steaks with buttermilk and cool for 4 hours. Remove the buffalo steaks, and pat dry with a paper towel. Coat the buffalo steaks in flour, and in a large cast iron skillet, fry them in butter to the tenderness and inside color you desire. Add the remaining ingredients, and simmer in skillet on low heat for about 15 minutes. Check for seasonings before serving. These are the steaks that make Fort Madison, Iowa, famous!

HIGH PLAINS DRIFTER BUFFALO LIVER

½ cup oil

1 whole bison liver, sliced

½ cup flour

1 cup water

2 cups beef stock

3 tablespoons tomato sauce

1 large yellow onion, sliced

2 garlic cloves, chopped

½ teaspoon oregano

½ tablespoon salt

1 tablespoon fresh ground black pepper

Heat the oil in a large, heavy skillet. Coat the bison liver slices in flour and brown in the skillet. Add the remaining flour to the skillet, then add 1 cup water. Preheat oven to 350 degrees. Remove the meat from the skillet, and in a large baking dish, add the cooked liver with all the remaining ingredients, and bake for about an hour. Check again for seasonings, and serve with mashed potatoes, using the gravy from the skillet.

CHIEF KEOKUK BUFFALO TONGUE

1 buffalo tongue

4 yellow onions, chopped

2 cups beef stock

2 garlic cloves, chopped

1 tablespoon seasoned salt

1 tablespoon fresh ground black pepper

Preheat the oven to 350 degrees. In a large pot, boil the buffalo tongue in salted water for about 30 minutes. Place the boiled tongue in a large baking dish, and add the remaining ingredients. Cover, and bake for 1 hour, or until the meat is tender. Slice and serve.

OPEN RANGE BUFFALO ROAST

1 large buffalo roast

3 tablespoons oil

6 potatoes, peeled and halved

1 onion, sliced

½ cup beef stock

1 tablespoon salt

1 tablespoon black pepper

1 tablespoon garlic powder

1 tablespoon onion powder

Preheat the oven to 350 degrees. In a large iron skillet, sear the buffalo roast on all sides in oil until browned. Place the buffalo roast and remaining ingredients in a large Dutch oven, and bake for about 1½ hours or until the veggies and meat are cooked and tender. Check again for seasonings, and serve.

COUSIN RICK'S BISON BURGERS

½ cup chopped onion

2 large dill pickles, chopped

1 tablespoon dill weed

¼ tablespoon hot sauce

1 tablespoon seasoned salt

1 pound ground buffalo meat

Sprinkle the chopped onions, pickles, dill weed, hot sauce, and salt over the ground buffalo meat. Mix together well, and form 4 large patties with the seasoned meat. Grill the buffalo meat patties for about 6 minutes per side, and season to taste with the seasoned salt. Serve grilled buffalo patties on toasted buns topped with your favorite veggies and sauce.

BOAR LOIN IN MUSTARD SAUCE

1 pound boneless boar loin chops

Quart-size zippered plastic bag

3 tablespoons wine vinegar

1 tablespoon Worcestershire sauce

1 tablespoon salad oil

2 garlic cloves, crushed

½ cup sour cream

2 tablespoons Dijon mustard

Place the boar loin chops in the zippered plastic bag. Combine the vinegar, Worcestershire sauce, salad oil, and crushed garlic cloves in a mixing bowl, and pour into the bag over boar meat. Marinate overnight in a cooler or icebox. When the meat is ready, grill it on each side over medium coals until fully cooked. Meanwhile, prepare the mustard sauce for on the side: Combine the sour cream and Dijon mustard, and chill until ready to serve with cooked boar.

COOKING WITH BUFFALO

To prepare buffalo (also called bison), treat it just like a cow: skin, gut, and remove the head. However, in my experience, cooking with buffalo can get a little trickier, as it has literally no fat (as is the case with most large game animals). It needs to be cooked very slowly (under 300 degrees) to keep the meat from drying out. I have found that roasting in a crockpot works well, as does a Dutch oven filled with vegetables to cover the meat and keep the moisture in. Most of my hunting buddies—Jeff May, Tod Larson, Josh Clark, and of course my son Travis—will cook buffalo mixed with beef to maintain moisture. This, however, only works in burgers and stews.

COOKING WITH WILD BOAR

Wild boar, along with feral hogs, are found in over 20 states and are estimated to number close to 3 million. Like domestic swine, these guys are not native to North America. Originally domesticated and then released into the wild, these creatures are now hybrids. Not only is wild boar fun to hunt, but the flavor is great when cooked correctly.

Best States to Hunt Wild Boar
- South Carolina
- Oklahoma
- Alabama
- Arkansas
- Louisiana
- Georgia
- Florida
- Texas

Hunter Stories

Bubba kept telling me and his other hunting buddies the same story,
and we chided him for telling it over and over.
He reminded us that we often tell the same stories.
"Not so," I said. "We re-share, you repeat."

COUSIN RICK'S GRILLING AND SMOKER WOOD TIPS

More and more outdoor cooks are enjoying the art of smoking and grilling their wild game. Let's face it, we hunters just love that wonderful, classic barbecue flavor that comes from the smoke of burning charcoal briquettes. Now, to enhance that flavor, some cooks are using aromatic smoking woods. The irresistible aroma of these woods penetrates the wild game meat and adds a great new taste to a piece of meat. My favorite varieties are mesquite, hickory, and, of course, the fruitwoods. So let's take a look at which woods will go best with the game you are going to smoke or grill.

Hickory

The most popular of all the hardwood flavorings, hickory is known for its strong, dense-flavored smoke. I use hickory with bison, venison, wild boar, and fish. Keep in mind, however, that hickory can leave a bitter taste in your game meat if not used correctly. Like all smoking woods, hickory needs to soak in water before use. I always give my smoking woods a minimum 2-hour water bath, and I highly recommend you do the same to ensure a full smoky flavor.

Mesquite

Mesquite is another popular grilling and smoking wood that is sweeter and more delicate than hickory. I use mesquite with the richly flavored game meats, such as duck, pheasant, turkey, mountain goat, and bear. However, just like hickory, mesquite can leave a bitter taste in your game if used incorrectly. As with hickory, always shoot for at least 2 hours of soaking in water.

Fruitwoods

Fruitwoods are steadily becoming more popular among us outdoor cooks. These woods, such as apple and cherry, are excellent with grilling and smoking all game birds, wild boar, and most small game.

In closing always remember: Aromatic smoking woods are not a replacement for charcoal, fire, or propane, the main sources of cooking heat.

WILD HOG BACON

BRINE:

2 gallons of water

2 cups sea salt

¼ cup curing salt (pink salt)

¼ cup whole peppercorns

¼ cup garlic powder

¼ cup onion powder

¼ cup Worcestershire sauce

1 cup brown sugar

MEAT:

2 good-sized wild boar bellies

Mix brine ingredients, and soak the boar belly for 2 days. Then, take the boar belly out, and rinse under cool water. Hang meat in a clean area, and dry with a fan until pellicle forms, about 1 hour. Cold smoke for 2 hours using apple wood chips. Freeze, slice thinly, and enjoy!

COUSIN RICK'S FAMILY WILD BOAR SALAMI RECIPE

2 pounds ground wild boar

¼ teaspoon garlic powder

¼ teaspoon onion powder

½ teaspoon mustard seed

2 tablespoons sugar-based curing mixture (such as Tender Quick)

1 tablespoon coarsely ground black pepper

1 teaspoon liquid smoke flavoring

1 teaspoon red pepper flakes (optional)

In a large bowl, mix together the ground wild boar meat, garlic powder, onion powder, mustard seed, curing mixture, black pepper, and liquid smoke. Mix in the red pepper flakes too, if desired. Roll the mixture into a 2-inch-diameter log, and wrap tightly in aluminum foil. Refrigerate for 24 hours. Preheat the oven to 325 degrees. Make a few slits in the bottom of the roll to allow the fat to drain when cooking. Place roll onto a broiler pan, and fill the bottom part of the pan with about 1 inch of water to keep the salami moist. Bake for 90 minutes in oven. Remove from pan, and cool completely before unwrapping the salami. This makes a great Christmas gift!

WILD BOAR SHANKS

¼ cup canola oil

6 wild boar shanks

12 garlic cloves, lightly smashed

8 star anise pods

3 whole cloves

Two (4-inch) cinnamon sticks

10 cups water

1 cup low-sodium soy sauce

2 tablespoons molasses

1 cup light brown sugar

In a very large skillet, heat the oil. Add the boar shanks in a single layer, and cook over moderately high heat, turning occasionally, until browned, about 10 minutes. Transfer the shanks to a large Dutch oven. Add the garlic, star anise, cloves, and cinnamon sticks to the Dutch oven, and cook over low heat, stirring occasionally, until fragrant. Add the water along with soy sauce, molasses, and sugar, and scrape up any bits stuck to the pan. Pour in the liquid, and bring to a boil. Simmer over low heat, partially covered, until the meat is tender and nearly falling off the bone, about 2 hours, turning the shanks occasionally. Transfer the shanks to shallow bowls, and strain the broth. Spoon off as much fat as possible. Check for seasonings, and serve with wild rice.

SLOW-COOKED MOOSE ROAST

4 pounds moose roast

Salt to taste

Ground black pepper to taste

1 packet dry onion soup mix

1 cup water

3 carrots, chopped

1 onion, chopped

3 potatoes, peeled and cubed

1 stalk celery, chopped

Season the moose roast with salt and pepper to taste. Brown on all sides in a large skillet over high heat, about 4 minutes per side. Place the moose roast in a slow cooker, and add the soup mix, along with 1 cup water, carrots, onion, potatoes, and celery. Cover and cook on low for 8 to 10 hours. Check for seasonings, and serve hot. Very good with cornbread!

MOOSE JERKY

¾ cup Worcestershire sauce
¾ cup soy sauce
1 tablespoon smoked paprika (or to taste)
1 tablespoon honey (or more to taste)
2 teaspoons freshly ground black pepper

1 teaspoon red pepper flakes
1 teaspoon garlic powder
1 teaspoon onion powder
2 pounds moose roast, thinly sliced

Whisk Worcestershire sauce, soy sauce, paprika, honey, black pepper, red pepper flakes, garlic powder, and onion powder together in a bowl. Add moose meat slices to bowl, and turn to coat moose completely. Cover the bowl with plastic wrap, and marinate in the refrigerator, 3 hours to overnight. Preheat oven to 175 degrees. Line a baking sheet with aluminum foil, and place a wire rack over the foil. Transfer moose to paper towels to dry. Discard marinade. Arrange moose slices in a single layer on the prepared wire rack on the baking sheet. Bake the moose slices in oven until dry and leathery, 3 to 4 hours. Cut with scissors into bite-size pieces.

MOOSE DUTCH OVEN STEW

4 pounds moose roast, cut into 2-inch pieces
½ teaspoons kosher salt
1 teaspoon freshly ground black pepper
3 tablespoons all-purpose flour
1 tablespoon olive oil
¼ cup tomato paste
2 cups dry red wine

4 cups chicken broth
1 medium yellow onion, quartered
2 bay leaves
4 sprigs thyme
10 carrots, peeled and cut into 3-inch pieces
1½ pounds red potatoes, halved

Preheat the oven to 325 degrees. Season the moose meat with salt and pepper, place in a large bowl, and toss with the flour. Heat the oil in a large Dutch oven over medium-high heat. Cook the moose meat, in batches, until well browned on all sides, and then set aside. Pour off, and discard any drippings from the pot. Add the tomato paste, wine, broth, onion, bay leaves, thyme, and half the carrots, and bring to a boil. Return the meat and any juices back to the Dutch oven, and cover, then transfer to the oven. Cook for 2 hours. Using tongs, remove and discard the cooked vegetables. Add the potatoes and the remaining 5 carrots to the Dutch oven, cover, and return to the oven. Cook for about 1 hour or until the meat is tender, as well as the veggies. Check for seasonings, and serve.

MOOSE STEAK FANCY CAMP

2 medium-size moose steaks
1 tablespoon butter
¼ cup brandy
1 onion, minced
1 clove garlic, minced
½ cup red wine
2 tablespoons steak sauce

1 dash Worcestershire sauce
Salt to taste
Ground black pepper to taste
½ (4-ounce) package button mushrooms, sliced
½ cup Dijon mustard, divided
1 cup heavy cream

Place the moose steaks between two sheets of plastic wrap; pound with a kitchen mallet to tenderize. Melt the butter in a skillet over medium-high heat, and heat until it begins to smoke. Cook the moose steaks until browned. Pour brandy over steaks, and carefully ignite. Once the flames burn off, remove moose steaks from the pan, and set aside. Cook the onion and garlic in the same skillet over medium heat until they soften. Stir in the red wine, steak sauce, Worcestershire sauce, salt, and pepper; mix well. Add in the mushrooms, stir, and cook for about 5 minutes. Meanwhile, coat one side of each of the moose steaks with 2 tablespoons of the Dijon mustard. Gently lay them on top of the sauce in the skillet, mustard-side down. Spread 2 more tablespoons mustard on top of the steaks. Cook 2 to 3 minutes per side. Remove the steaks from the sauce, and keep warm. Stir the cream into the mushroom sauce, and bring to a gentle simmer. Reduce heat to medium-low, return the steaks to the sauce, and simmer for about 5 minutes. Check for seasonings before serving.

BULLWINKLE BURGERS

1 tablespoon canola oil
2 cups thinly sliced sweet onion
¼ teaspoon seasoned salt
¾ cup beer
2 pounds ground lean ground moose

2 tablespoons soy sauce
¼ teaspoon ground black pepper
4 slices Swiss cheese
8 teaspoons spicy brown mustard
4 hamburger buns, toasted

Heat oil in a large skillet over medium-high heat. Add onion and seasoned salt; cook until tender, stirring occasionally. Carefully add beer. Bring to a boil. Reduce heat, cover, and simmer 10 minutes, stirring occasionally. Remove lid, and simmer 5 minutes more or until liquid has evaporated. Meanwhile, combine moose, soy sauce, and pepper in a medium bowl. Shape mixture into 4 patties, about ½-inch thick. Heat another large skillet over medium-high heat. Add patties; cook 5 minutes on each side or until cooked through. Top each patty with 1 slice cheese; melt slightly. Remove from heat. Spread 2 teaspoons mustard on bottom half of each bun. Top each with a moose patty and about ¼ cup onion mixture. Close with tops of buns, check for seasonings, and serve hot.

COOKING WITH MOOSE

Moose is one of the most richly flavored big game meats. Like other wild game, moose's flavor and tenderness will vary widely depending on its diet, its habitat, how clean the kill was, and how quickly the hunter cleaned and chilled the carcass. Most of the meat will be relatively tough, though the loin and rib sections will yield very tasty roasts.

About Moose Meat

If you have been on a moose hunt, you'll know that moose are at their well-fed peak in the fall, after building their winter stores of fat. If a moose is especially strong in flavor, you may want to marinate it for at least 48 hours before roasting it. Traditional marinades for moose usually include red wine, onions, bay leaves, garlic, and black peppercorns, as well as other flavoring ingredients such as juniper berries or red currants.

Best States to Hunt Moose

- Alaska
- Maine
- Idaho
- Washington

©2016 Dan Roberts

"Ghillie suit?
I thought you said to wear a Gilligan suit."

MOOSE POT PIE

1 pound moose steak, cubed

Salt to taste

Ground black pepper to taste

1 can beef broth

3 large carrots, diced

3 potatoes, cubed

1 cup frozen green peas, thawed

3 tablespoons cornstarch

1/3 cup water

2 (9-inch) pie crusts

In a saucepan over medium heat, brown the pieces of moose meat on all sides. Pour in some water to almost cover. Bring to a boil, and reduce heat. Simmer until the moose meat is tender and falls apart easily, about 3 hours. Transfer moose meat to a large mixing bowl. Shred the meat slightly, and add salt and pepper to taste. In another large saucepan over medium heat, pour in beef broth, and add carrots and potatoes. Cook until almost tender, about 15 to 20 minutes. Preheat oven to 350 degrees. When the carrots and potatoes are tender, transfer to the large mixing bowl with the cooked moose meat, leaving the liquid in the pan. Combine the peas with the carrots, potatoes, and meat. Dissolve the cornstarch with the 1/3 cup of water. Pour into the saucepan of beef broth, stirring constantly. Bring to a simmer and reduce heat; cook for 5 minutes. Line a 9-inch pie plate with one of the crusts, following the package directions. Place the moose meat mixture into the crust. Pour gravy over the top of the mixture, then cover with the other pie crust. Bake in oven until the crust is golden brown, about 25 minutes. Let cool for 5 minutes before serving.

QUICK AND EASY CARIBOU TENDERLOINS

1 (3-pound) caribou tenderloin roast

3/4 cup soy sauce

1/2 cup melted butter

Preheat oven to 350 degrees. Place the caribou roast into a shallow, glass baking dish. Pour soy sauce and melted butter over the tenderloin. Bake in oven for 10 minutes, then turn the caribou roast over, and continue cooking 35 to 40 minutes, basting occasionally. Cook to your desired degree of doneness. Let the caribou meat rest for 10 to 15 minutes before slicing.

CARIBOU CAMP LOAF

2 bay leaves

1 teaspoon salt

1 teaspoon ground cayenne pepper

1 teaspoon ground black pepper

½ teaspoon ground white pepper

½ teaspoon ground cumin

½ teaspoon ground nutmeg

4 tablespoons butter

¾ cup chopped onion

½ cup chopped green bell pepper

¼ cup chopped green onions

4 cloves garlic, minced

1 tablespoon Louisiana hot sauce

1 tablespoon Worcestershire sauce

½ cup evaporated milk

½ cup ketchup

2 pounds ground caribou meat

½ pound andouille sausage

2 eggs, beaten

1 cup dried bread crumbs

In a small bowl, combine the bay leaves, salt, cayenne pepper, black pepper, white pepper, cumin, and nutmeg; set aside. Melt the butter in a saucepan over medium heat. Add the onion, bell pepper, green onions, garlic, hot sauce, Worcestershire sauce, and the seasoning mix from the small bowl. Sauté until mixture starts sticking to the bottom of the pan. Stir in the evaporated milk and ketchup; continue cooking on low heat for 5 more minutes, stirring occasionally. Remove vegetable mixture from heat, and allow to cool to room temperature. Place the caribou and sausage in an ungreased 9- by 13-inch baking dish. Add the eggs, the vegetable mixture, and the bread crumbs. Remove the bay leaves. Mix well, and form into a loaf. Bake uncovered at 350 degrees for 30 minutes. Then raise heat to 425 degrees, and bake for another 35 minutes. Let stand for at least 5 minutes before serving.

COUSIN RICK'S BEST CARIBOU LIVER

2 pounds caribou liver, sliced

1½ cups milk

¼ cup salted butter, divided

2 large onions, sliced into rings

2 cups flour

Salt to taste

Ground black pepper to taste

Gently rinse the caribou liver slices under cold water, and place in a bowl. Pour in enough milk to cover. Let stand for 1 hour. Melt 2 tablespoons of butter in a large cast iron skillet over medium heat. Separate onion rings, and sauté them in butter until tender. Remove onions, and melt remaining butter in the skillet. Season the flour with salt and pepper, and place in a shallow dish. Drain milk from caribou liver, and coat slices in the flour mixture. When the butter has melted, turn the heat up to medium-high, and place the coated caribou liver slices in the pan. Cook until caribou is brown on the bottom. Turn, and cook on the other side until browned. Add onions, and reduce heat to medium. Simmer caribou liver on low for another 20 minutes. Check for seasonings, and serve.

CARIBOU RIB ROAST

1 large caribou rib roast	1 teaspoon ground black pepper
2 teaspoons seasoned salt	1 teaspoon garlic powder

Allow caribou roast to stand at room temperature for at least 1 hour. Preheat the oven to 375 degrees. Combine the seasoned salt, pepper, and garlic powder in a small bowl. Place the caribou roast on a rack in a roasting pan so that the rib side is on the bottom. Rub the seasoning onto the caribou roast. Roast for 1 hour in oven. Turn the oven temperature down to 150 degrees, and keep the caribou roast warm and slow bake for about 3 hours. When it's 30 minutes before serving, turn the oven back up to 375 degrees to reheat the caribou roast. The internal temperature should be at least 150 degrees. Remove from the oven, and let rest for 15 minutes before serving.

HEARTY OUTDOORSMAN CARIBOU STEAK

2-inch thick caribou steak, at room temperature	Hickory wood chips, soaked in water for at least 2 hours
Seasoned salt to taste	Olive oil
Freshly ground black pepper to taste	

Season the caribou steak generously with salt and black pepper on both sides. Place wood chips in the smoker box of your smoke vault. Preheat one side of the grill to about 225 degrees. Place caribou steak on the cool side of the grill. Cook for about 1 hour, then transfer the caribou steak to a serving plate. Brush with olive oil, and cover with aluminum foil. Increase heat on the grill to 650 degrees by turning all burners up to maximum. Cook the caribou steak until a crust forms, about 5 minutes per side. Transfer steak back to the serving plate. Let stand for about 10 minutes, and serve.

Short Season

On the first day of the hunting season,
Bubba fell out of a stand and broke both his legs.

"Why couldn't this have happened on my last day of hunting?!"
he cried to his doctor.

The doctor took one look at Bubba's legs and shook his head. "It did."

COOKING WITH CARIBOU

Caribou is one of the healthiest red meats you can eat—it's lean, smooth, and simply delicious! Its meat is finely grained and resembles veal or antelope in flavor and texture.

Alaska is the best state for hunting caribou. If looking at going out of the United States, Canada is a good, economical option.

COOKING WITH ELK

The second-largest member of the deer family, elk are very dark and coarsely grained. They can be described as the sweetest of the deer meats—very tender and succulent. For this reason, elk can be cooked in much the same way as venison.

Best States to Hunt Elk

- Colorado
- Utah
- Oregon
- Pennsylvania
- Arizona
- Washington
- New Mexico
- Wyoming
- Montana
- Idaho

ANSWERING NATURE'S CALL

We've all heard that if you leave your stand to answer nature's call on the ground below, you may as well find a new spot to hunt. My hunting pals and I have found that the smell of human urine does not noticeably affect deer, if it affects them at all. For a research project with penned deer, the researchers sprayed all sorts of things into scrapes to see which deer liked best. In one sample, they used four things—buck urine, doe-in-estrous urine, human urine, and car air freshener. Results? With bucks, doe-in-estrous was the most popular, followed by human urine, then car air freshener, then buck urine. So stay as scent free as possible, and don't turn the ground near your stand into a urinal, but if you have to go, just go, and keep hunting.

CARIBOU JERKY STICKS

5 pounds ground caribou

1 pound spicy pork sausage

3 teaspoons mustard seed

2½ teaspoons liquid smoke flavoring

2 tablespoons Worcestershire sauce

1 tablespoon garlic powder

6 tablespoons sugar-based curing mixture

1 tablespoon cracked black pepper

1 tablespoon caraway seed

2 teaspoons cayenne pepper

2 teaspoons paprika

2 teaspoons chili powder

2 teaspoons red pepper flakes

In a large bowl, mix together the ground caribou meat, pork sausage, mustard seed, liquid smoke, Worcestershire sauce, garlic powder, curing mixture, black pepper, caraway seed, cayenne pepper, paprika, chili powder, and red pepper flakes. Cover, and refrigerate overnight. For the next 4 days, knead the meat for 5 minutes each day, then return to the refrigerator/cooler. On the 5th day, knead the meat, then form it into 8 equal logs. Preheat the oven to 210 degrees. Wrap each caribou log in aluminum foil, and poke a few holes in the foil. Place the logs onto a broiler pan to catch the grease. Bake for 6 hours, then turn off the oven, and leave the logs in for another 2½ hours. Refrigerate until chilled, then slice into serving-size pieces. These jerky sticks are another great gift for your hunting posse!

"Whew! Cousin Rick's new cookbook doesn't have any recipes for Bigfoots in it!"

ELK CAMP STEAK MEAL

2 pounds elk steak

1 green bell pepper

2 tablespoons vegetable oil

1 (29-ounce) can diced tomatoes

¼ cup soy sauce

½ teaspoon garlic powder

½ teaspoon ground black pepper

½ teaspoon ground ginger

1 beef bouillon cube

4 tablespoons cornstarch

2 cups water

RICE:

2 cups water

1 cup white rice

Trim any fat from the elk steak, and slice the elk meat into thin, 2- to 3-inch-long strips. Remove the seeds and core from the green bell pepper, and slice into thin, 3-inch-long strips. In a large cast iron frying pan over medium to high heat, add oil, and cook meat until medium rare. Add peppers, and continue cooking until elk meat is browned. Reduce heat to a simmer, and add tomatoes, soy sauce, garlic powder, black pepper, and ginger. Cover, and simmer 10 minutes. Dissolve bouillon cube and cornstarch in 2 cups water, and stir well before adding to simmering elk. Cover, and simmer 10 minutes, stirring occasionally, until sauce resembles the consistency of gravy. Remove from heat, and serve over a bed of rice. To cook rice: In a saucepan, bring 2 cups of water to a boil. Stir in 1 cup of rice. Cover, and reduce heat to a simmer. Simmer for 20 minutes.

ELK TATTERS AND GRAVY VITTLES

2 pounds thin-cut elk steak

1 (10.75-ounce) can condensed
cream of mushroom soup

1 (10.5-ounce) can condensed French onion soup

Salt to taste

Fresh ground black pepper to taste

10.75 ounces water

Preheat oven to 325 degrees. Trim any fat from the elk steak, and cut into desired number of servings. In a roasting pan over medium-high heat, sear both sides of the elk steak, about 1 minute per side. Remove from heat. Stir the cream of mushroom soup, French onion soup, and water (use the mushroom soup can to add 10.75 ounces of water) into the roaster. Bake for 2½ hours. Season to taste with salt and fresh ground black pepper.

ELK HUNT TRIGGER FINGERS

1 large elk steak

2 eggs

½ cup milk

Salt to taste

Ground black pepper to taste

⅓ cup vegetable oil

1½ cups all-purpose flour for coating

Tenderize the elk steak by pounding with a mallet. Cut into 3-inch-long strips. Combine eggs, milk, salt, and pepper in a shallow dish, whisk until well blended. In a large skillet over medium heat, heat ⅓ cup oil (or just enough to cover the bottom of the pan). Coat the elk steak pieces in flour, and then shake off excess. Dip pieces in the egg mixture and again in flour. Fry the strips in the hot oil until golden brown, about 2 minutes. Transfer to a basket or plate lined with paper towels to absorb oil. Season to taste, and serve.

CAMP OVEN BBQ ELK

5 pounds elk round steak, cut into 1-inch strips

2 tablespoons vegetable oil

1 clove garlic, minced

¾ cup distilled white vinegar

1 tablespoon sugar

½ cup ketchup

1 teaspoon dry mustard

1 teaspoon paprika

1 teaspoon salt

⅛ teaspoon black pepper

Preheat oven to 325 degrees. Heat oil in a large iron skillet over medium heat. Brown elk steak strips on all sides. Transfer strips to a baking dish. Stir garlic into skillet; cook 5 minutes. Add vinegar, sugar, and ketchup. Then stir in mustard, paprika, salt, and pepper; simmer 3 minutes. Pour sauce over elk steak strips. Cover baking dish, and bake for 1 hour. Uncover, and bake 30 minutes more. Check for seasonings, and serve hot.

Nice Try

On the way home from a hunt, Bubba stopped by the grocery store.

"Give me a couple of steaks," he said.

"We're out of steaks but we have hotdogs and chicken," said the butcher.

"Hotdogs and chicken?!" said Bubba. "How can I tell my wife I bagged a couple of hotdogs and chickens?"

JEFF GOT "PICKLED" ELK STEAK

12 dill pickle spears

1 large onion, sliced and halved

3 medium-size elk round steaks, cut into 4 pieces and
pounded thin

Toothpicks

¼ cup vegetable oil

½ cup all-purpose flour

2 eggs, beaten

3 (10.75-ounce) cans condensed cream of mushroom
soup, undiluted

Preheat oven to 350 degrees. Lightly grease a medium baking dish. Place one pickle spear and an equal amount of halved onion slices on one side of each piece of elk steak. Roll, and secure with toothpicks. Heat the oil in a skillet over medium heat. Place the flour and eggs in 2 separate bowls. Dip rolled elk steak first in the eggs, then in the flour to coat. Fry coated elk steaks in the skillet until browned on all sides. Transfer to the baking dish. Pour cream of mushroom soup into the skillet, and scrape up browned bits. Pour evenly over the elk steaks in the baking dish. Bake 45 minutes to a minimum internal temperature of 160 degrees, and serve.

MOMMA IT'S HOT! ELK STEAK

2 tablespoons olive oil

1½ pounds elk steak, cubed

3 cloves garlic, minced

½ cup chopped onion

4 habanero peppers, seeded and minced

½ cup tomato sauce

1 cup water (plus another ⅔ cup for the sauce)

2 tablespoons finely grated raw horseradish

1 tablespoon hot pepper sauce

2 tablespoons distilled white vinegar

1 tablespoon prepared yellow mustard

½ teaspoon seasoned salt

½ teaspoon ground black pepper

⅓ cup all-purpose flour

Heat the olive oil in a large saucepan over medium-high heat. Brown the elk steak cubes in the hot oil until well browned on all sides, about 8 minutes. Add in the garlic, onion, and minced habanero peppers. Cook and stir for a few minutes until the onion has begun to soften. Stir in the tomato sauce, 1 cup of water, horseradish, hot pepper sauce, vinegar, mustard, seasoned salt, and black pepper. Bring to a simmer, then reduce heat to medium-low, cover, and simmer until the elk begins to turn tender, about 2 hours. Stir occasionally. Dissolve the flour into ⅔ cup of cold water, and stir into the simmering meat. Cook until the meat is very tender and the sauce is thick and smooth, about 30 minutes more.

COLORADO ELK ROAST

4 pounds elk rump roast
1 (10.75-ounce) can condensed cream of mushroom
soup
1 (1-ounce) package dry onion soup mix

½ cup Burgundy wine
2 tablespoons all-purpose flour
1 (8-ounce) jar sliced mushrooms, drained (optional)

Preheat oven to 300 degrees. Place a large sheet of heavy-duty aluminum foil in a shallow roasting pan, and place elk roast in the pan. Pour mushroom soup over the elk roast, and sprinkle with onion soup mix. Whisk wine and flour together in a small bowl; pour over the elk roast, and top with mushrooms if desired. Fold the foil over the roast, and crimp the edges together to seal. Bake in oven for 4½ hours. Let stand for 10 minutes before serving.

HOLIDAY ELK ROAST

5 pounds elk roast
Salt to taste
Ground black pepper to taste
3 tablespoons butter, divided
½ cup water (plus another ½ cup for thickening the
sauce)
½ teaspoon dried sage
½ teaspoon dried mint

1 medium onion, sliced (optional)
1 clove garlic, minced (optional)
$\frac{1}{8}$ teaspoon seasoned salt (optional)
$\frac{1}{8}$ teaspoon red pepper flakes (optional)
1 tablespoon all-purpose flour
¼ teaspoon dried sage (plus more for seasoning)
¼ teaspoon dried mint (plus more for seasoning)

Preheat the oven to 350 degrees. Season the elk roast with salt and pepper to taste. Melt 2 tablespoons butter in a Dutch oven over medium-high heat. Brown the outside of the elk roast on all sides in the butter. After the elk roast is browned, add ½ cup water to the pan, and sprinkle ½ teaspoon of sage, and ½ teaspoon of mint onto the roast. Place onion and garlic into the pan if desired, and season with seasoned salt and red pepper flakes, if using. Cover the pot, and place the elk roast in the oven for 2 to 3 hours, depending on how well-done you prefer the meat to be (2 hours for rare, 3 for well done). Removed finished roast to a pan to keep warm. Melt remaining 1 tablespoon of butter in a medium skillet. Whisk flour into melted butter until smooth. Remove from heat, and stir in ½ cup cold water. Mix until a smooth paste is formed. Return to medium heat, and season with additional sage and mint. Stir in the liquid from the roasting pan, and boil, stirring constantly until the gravy is thickened. Remove from heat. Slice the elk roast, and serve with gravy poured over the meat.

ANTELOPE STEAKS

¼ cup Worcestershire sauce

2 tablespoons soy sauce

½ lime, juiced

1 tablespoon dried minced onion

1 teaspoon red pepper flakes

1 teaspoon dry mustard

½ teaspoon kosher salt

¼ teaspoon thyme

¼ teaspoon ground black pepper

¼ teaspoon dried, minced garlic

1 teaspoon Tabasco

2 medium-size antelope steaks

Whisk Worcestershire sauce, soy sauce, lime juice, onion, red pepper flakes, dry mustard, salt, thyme, black pepper, garlic, and Tabasco together in a bowl; pour into a resealable plastic bag. Add antelope steaks, coat with the marinade, squeeze to remove excess air, and seal the bag. Marinate in the refrigerator at least 1 hour. Preheat an outdoor grill for medium-high heat, and lightly oil the grate. Remove antelope from the marinade, and shake off excess. Discard remaining marinade. Cook the antelope steaks until they are firm, hot in the center, and just turning from pink to gray, about 5 minutes per side. An instant-read thermometer inserted into the center should read 150 degrees. Check for seasonings, and serve!

JACK DANIEL'S ANTELOPE

4 antelope strap steaks

1 cup Jack Daniel's

Seasoned salt to taste

Fresh ground pepper to taste

Garlic powder to taste

Place the antelope steaks in a nonmetallic dish, and pour the bourbon over the meat; turn to coat. Cover, and marinate in the refrigerator for at least 8 hours. Preheat grill for high heat. Brush grate with oil, and arrange the antelope steaks. Cook for 6 to 10 minutes. Turn, and cook until done to your liking, another 6 to 10 minutes. Season the antelope with seasoned salt, pepper, and garlic powder, and serve.

Cousin Rick's Deer Camp Quickies

Q: What do you get when you cross Bambi with a ghost?

A: Bamboo.

Q: Why did the hunter miss his mark?

A: He was not aiming deerectly.

ANTELOPE HUNTERS' STEW

2 tablespoons vegetable oil, divided

1 yellow onion, chopped

3 cloves garlic, minced

1 cup flour

1 teaspoon garlic powder

1 teaspoon garlic salt

2½ to 3 pounds antelope roast, cut into 1-inch pieces

4 cups beef broth

1 cup dry red wine

3 ounces tomato paste

1 tablespoon chopped fresh sage

1 bay leaf

2 cups parsnips cut into 1-inch pieces

2 cups carrots cut into 1-inch pieces

2 cups small quartered potatoes

1 tablespoon red wine vinegar

1 tablespoon fresh squeezed lemon

Salt to taste

Fresh ground black pepper to taste

¼ cup chopped fresh flat-leaf parsley

Heat a large cast iron skillet over medium heat, and add 1 tablespoon oil. Add onions and garlic, and sauté until onions soften. Transfer onions to a slow cooker. Add flour, garlic powder, and garlic salt to a zippered plastic bag. Toss cubed antelope meat to lightly coat, shake excess off, and set aside. Heat remaining 1 tablespoon oil over medium heat, and sear meat until golden brown. Transfer the antelope meat to the slow cooker. Carefully deglaze pan with beef broth and red wine, stirring with a wooden spoon until all crispy bits from bottom of pan are scraped up. Stir in the tomato paste, and pour liquid over antelope meat. Add sage and bay leaf to slow cooker. Cook on low, covered, for 4 hours. Add parsnips, carrots, potatoes, and vinegar. Cover and cook for an additional 2 to 3 hours, until the antelope meat is tender and vegetables are soft. Before serving, stir in lemon juice, season with salt and pepper, and garnish with chopped flat-leaf parsley.

"Are you sure we're going to catch more turkeys for Thanksgiving by wearing these Pilgrim costumes, Cousin?"

COOKING WITH ANTELOPE

Antelope look like deer, but they are actually members of a family that includes goats and oxen. Mild-tasting and finely grained, antelope meat is similar to venison and has only one-third the calories of beef. The pronghorn antelope is the second-fastest land mammal in the world, with the ability to reach speeds of more than 53 miles per hour. Hunters from around the world pursue antelope on the plains of western and central North America. After a successful antelope hunt, they prepare the meat–commonly referred to as venison–in a variety of ways, including as sausages, jerky, steaks, and roasts. Grilling a lean antelope steak, however, is one of the most delicious and easiest ways to cook venison.

Best States to Hunt Antelope

- New Mexico
- Arizona
- Nevada
- Montana
- Colorado
- Texas
- Oregon

ANTELOPE CHILI VITTLES

2 pounds ground antelope steak or roast

1 pound bulk Italian sausage

3 (15-ounce) cans chili beans, drained

1 (15-ounce) can chili beans in spicy sauce

2 (28-ounce) cans diced tomatoes with juice

1 (6-ounce) can tomato paste

1 large yellow onion, chopped

3 stalks celery, chopped

1 green bell pepper, seeded and chopped

1 red bell pepper, seeded and chopped

2 green chili peppers, seeded and chopped

1 tablespoon bacon bits

4 cubes beef bouillon

½ cup beer

¼ cup chili powder

1 tablespoon Worcestershire sauce

1 tablespoon minced garlic

1 tablespoon dried oregano

2 teaspoons ground cumin

2 teaspoons Tabasco

1 teaspoon dried basil

1 teaspoon salt

1 teaspoon ground black pepper

1 teaspoon cayenne pepper

1 teaspoon paprika

1 teaspoon sugar

Heat a large stockpot over medium-high heat. Crumble the ground antelope and sausage into the hot pan, and cook until evenly browned. Drain off excess grease. Pour in the chili beans, spicy chili beans, diced tomatoes, and tomato paste. Add the onion, celery, green and red bell peppers, chili peppers, bacon bits, bouillon, and beer. Season with chili powder, Worcestershire sauce, garlic, oregano, cumin, Tabasco, basil, salt, pepper, cayenne, paprika, and sugar. Stir to blend, then cover and simmer over low heat for at least 2 hours, stirring occasionally. After 2 hours, taste, and adjust salt, pepper, and chili powder if necessary.

CHEF SAGE ISLAND-STYLE ANTELOPE BURGER

DOUGH:

2 cups all-purpose flour	¼ cup margarine
1½ teaspoons curry powder	¼ cup shortening
Pinch of salt	⅓ cup water

SANDWICH FILLING:

2 tablespoons margarine	1 teaspoon salt
1 small onion, finely diced	1 teaspoon pepper
1 pound ground antelope meat	½ cup beef broth
1 teaspoon curry powder	½ cup dry bread crumbs
1 teaspoon dried thyme	1 egg, beaten

Preheat oven to 400 degrees. In a large bowl, combine flour, curry powder, and salt. Cut in margarine and shortening until mixture resembles coarse crumbs. Stir in water until mixture forms a ball. Shape dough into a log, and cut into 10 equal sections. Roll each section into a 6-inch circle (approximately ⅛-inch thick). Set aside. Melt margarine in a skillet over medium heat. Sauté onion until soft and translucent. Stir in antelope. Season with curry powder, thyme, salt, and pepper. Cook until the antelope is evenly brown, stirring constantly. Stir in beef broth and bread crumbs. Simmer until liquid is absorbed. Remove from heat. Spoon equal amounts of filling into each pastry circle. Fold over, and press edges together, making a half circle. Use a fork to press edges, and brush the top of each packet with beaten egg. Bake in oven for 30 minutes, or until golden brown. I never would've guessed in 100 years that I'd have one of the best-tasting antelope sandwiches ever in Montego Bay, Jamaica, but Chef Sage cooked this wonderful treat for my wife and I, using antelope he got from a friend in Europe.

COOKING WITH DEER: WHITETAIL, BLACKTAIL, AND MULE DEER

When it comes to deer hunting and cooking with venison, I could write a book on it—in fact, I did! I'm going to share some of my best recipes for whitetail, blacktail, and mulies. Enjoy!

Best States to Hunt Whitetail
- Wisconsin
- Illinois
- Iowa
- Minnesota
- Kentucky
- Ohio
- Missouri
- Kansas
- Texas

Best States to Hunt Blacktail
- California
- Oregon
- Washington

Best States to Hunt Mule Deer
- Arizona
- Colorado
- Idaho
- Montana

Well, There's Your Answer

Bubba was telling me he just messed up another deer hunt.
This had happened to him more times than he could count.
He would spot a buck, aim, fire, and miss.
He would try to sneak up close, only to get busted and watch the deer run away.
As soon as the buck came into range, he'd sneeze and scare it away.
Either that, or he'd fall asleep on stand, waking just in time to watch a giant buck scamper away. Frustrated, he complained to me: "Everything that happens to guys that don't know how to hunt keeps happening to me!"

DEER CAMP LOINS AND SHALLOTS

¾ pound shallots, halved lengthwise and peeled

2 tablespoons olive oil

Salt to taste

Ground black pepper to taste

3 cups beef stock

¾ cup white wine

2 teaspoons tomato paste

2 pounds venison tenderloin roast, trimmed

1 teaspoon dried thyme

3 slices bacon, diced

3 tablespoons butter, divided

1 tablespoon all-purpose flour

4 sprigs watercress, for garnish

Preheat oven to 375 degrees. In a medium baking pan, toss shallots with oil to coat. Season with salt and pepper. Roast until shallots are deep brown and very tender, stirring occasionally. In a large saucepan, combine beef stock and wine. Bring to a boil. Cook over high heat until reduced by half, about 30 minutes. Whisk in tomato paste. Set aside. Pat venison dry; sprinkle with thyme, salt, and pepper. In a large roasting pan, set over medium heat on the stove top, sauté bacon until golden. Using a slotted wooden spoon, transfer bacon to paper towels. Add venison to pan; brown on all sides over medium-high heat, and transfer pan to oven. Roast venison until a meat thermometer inserted into center registers 125 degrees. Transfer the venison to a platter. Cover loosely with foil. Spoon fat off top of pan drippings in roasting pan. Place pan over high heat on stove top.

Add stock mixture, and bring to a boil; stir to scrape up any browned bits. Transfer to a medium saucepan, and bring to a simmer. Mix 1½ table-spoons butter and the flour in a small bowl to form a smooth paste; whisk into broth mix-ture, and simmer until sauce thickens. Whisk in remaining butter. Stir in roasted shallots and reserved bacon. Season with salt and pepper. Cut venison into ½-inch-thick slices. Spoon the sauce over, and garnish with watercress.

"SO WHICH OF THE SEASONINGS DO YOU WANT ME TO COOK YOU WITH?"

COUSIN RICK'S OUTSIDE-THE-BOX TIPS ON DEER HUNTING

- Get in shape! It can take enormous effort to climb through downed timber, creeks, and trails. Not to mention that if you bag and tag a big buck, you have to haul the animal out.
- Don't smoke. Tobacco smoke is not a natural scent to deer and makes them nervous. It will alert them to where you are sitting or standing.
- Never drink alcohol while you are hunting. It is illegal. Do yourself, the deer, and the other hunters a favor: leave it in camp. You can enjoy yourself and celebrate after the hunt.
- Wrap a small piece of plastic to the muzzle of your rifle, shotgun, or muzzleloader to keep dirt and moisture out of your barrel.
- When scouting, look at areas where you see deer sign, such as rubs and scrapes. Also look for deer runs.
- If you must pack out quarters and you have to leave portions in the field overnight, hang your meat from a tree. Coyotes and foxes will easily find your gut pile and your remaining meat, and a small pack of coyotes can make off with your quarters.
- Always sight in your hunting weapon every year to ensure it is shooting accurately. Know your weapon and your own shooting abilities, and do not take high-risk shots. Be a responsible hunter.
- Unfortunately, meth manufacturers and marijuana growers frequently use public land. If you see or walk into a site, clear out of the area as fast as you can and notify authorities.
- Keep your cell phone on but in silent mode. You don't want to lose a chance at that record buck because your wife called to check in on how things are going.
- Be legal. Have your tags, licenses, and permission from the landowner to hunt.

Cousin Rick's Deer Camp Quickies

Q: What do you call four female deer?

A: FO REAL DOE.

Q: What did the female deer say to her mate when he wanted a three-way?

A: It might be a buck more, but I wouldn't buy that for a dollar.

COUSIN RICK'S VENISON AND BROCCOLI

1/3 cup oyster sauce

2 teaspoons toasted sesame oil

1/3 cup sherry

1 teaspoon soy sauce

1 teaspoon sugar

1 teaspoon cornstarch

3/4 pound venison round steak,
cut into 1/8-inch-thick strips

3 tablespoons vegetable oil (plus more if needed)

1 thin slice of fresh ginger root

1 clove garlic, peeled and smashed

1 pound broccoli, cut into florets

Whisk together the oyster sauce, sesame oil, sherry, soy sauce, sugar, and cornstarch in a bowl, and stir until the sugar has dissolved. Place the deer steak pieces into a shallow bowl, pour the oyster sauce mixture over the meat, stir to coat well, and marinate for at least 30 minutes in the refrigerator. Heat vegetable oil in a wok or large skillet over medium-high heat, and stir in the ginger and garlic. Let them sizzle in the hot oil for about 1 minute to flavor the oil, then remove and discard. Stir in the broccoli, and toss and stir in the hot oil until bright green and almost tender, 5 to 7 minutes. Remove the broccoli from the wok, and set aside. Pour a little more oil into the wok if needed, and stir and toss the deer with the marinade until the sauce forms a glaze on the deer steak and the meat is no longer pink, about 5 minutes. Return the cooked broccoli to the wok, and stir until the meat and broccoli are heated through. Check for seasonings, and serve.

THE DUKE'S MUSTARD GRILLED DEER STEAK

1/4 cup sherry vinegar

1/4 cup light olive oil

2 tablespoons Dijon mustard

2 tablespoons smoked paprika

4 cloves garlic, minced (optional)

Salt to taste

Ground black pepper to taste

2 pounds very thin deer flank steak

Preheat an outdoor grill for high heat, and lightly oil the grate. Whisk sherry vinegar, olive oil, mustard, paprika, garlic, salt, and pepper together in a large bowl. Place deer steak in marinade, and turn to coat. Marinate at room temperature for 30 minutes. Cook deer steak on the preheated grill, turning once, until each side is browned, about 2 minutes per side. The steak should be beginning to firm, hot and slightly pink in the center. Transfer the deer steak to a plate, and let rest for 5 to 10 minutes before slicing. This is great tasting deer vittles!

CNH DEER K BOB'S

2 tablespoons beef bouillon granules

2 tablespoons water

3 cloves garlic, minced

2 teaspoons cayenne pepper

½ teaspoon salt

1 teaspoon black pepper

2 pounds deer steak, cut into ½-inch cubes

10 wooden skewers, soaked in water for 1 hour

2 tablespoons vegetable oil

Dissolve bouillon in water. Stir in the garlic, cayenne pepper, salt, and black pepper. Toss the deer meat in the marinade, cover, and marinate in the refrigerator for at least 2 hours. Preheat a grill for high heat. Skewer the deer cubes, using 6 to 8 pieces per skewer. Pour the oil onto a plate, and roll the skewers in it to coat the meat on all sides. Grill the skewers, turning frequently, until the deer meat has turned light pink, 12 to 15 minutes. I serve this with wild rice at deer camp, and it's an easy but great tasting meal.

NO VAMPS AT CAMP STEAK

8 cloves garlic, minced

1 tablespoon olive oil

Salt to taste

Ground black pepper to taste

2 large deer steaks

12 cloves garlic, peeled

1 cup olive oil for frying

1½ tablespoons balsamic vinegar

Whisk minced garlic, olive oil, a pinch of salt, and a pinch of black pepper in a bowl, then pour into a zippered plastic bag. Add the deer steaks, coat with the marinade, squeeze out excess air, and seal the bag. Marinate in the refrigerator for at least 8 hours or overnight. Combine 12 garlic cloves and 1 cup olive oil in a small saucepan over low heat. Cook, stirring occasionally, until garlic is golden and tender, about 30 minutes. Set aside. Preheat an outdoor grill for high heat, and lightly oil the grate. Remove the deer steaks from bag, and wipe off excess marinade with paper towels. Generously season deer steaks with salt and black pepper. Cook the deer steaks on the prepared grill until they start to firm and are reddish-pink and juicy in the center, about 5 minutes per side. Remove steaks to a plate, and let rest for 5 to 8 minutes. Drizzle balsamic vinegar over steaks, then spoon a few cloves of oil-roasted garlic on top. This is full of flavor, but don't expect any loving from momma when you get back from the deer hunt with all that garlic on your breath. Ha!

COUSIN RICK'S GRILLED DEER ROAST

3 pounds or so deer roast (thawed)

2 tablespoons Thompson No Salt Seasoning Blend

⅓ cup apple cider vinegar

2 tablespoons extra virgin olive oil

2 tablespoons tamari soy sauce

1 tablespoon Worcestershire sauce

1 tablespoon dry mustard

½ tablespoon black pepper

½ tablespoon garlic powder

½ tablespoon sea salt

Rub both sides of the deer roast with the organic no-salt seasoning blend. Place it in a baking dish. Mix all the other ingredients in a prep bowl, and blend well. Pour mixture over the deer roast (careful not to wash all of the rub off), then lift the corner of the roast so that you also get marinade under it. Set it back down in the pan, then place the pan in the refrigerator. Allow it to marinate for at least 4 hours, turning it over about every hour. Prep the grill for smoking (around 185 degrees). When the temperature is stable, put the deer roast on, and let it smoke for 30 minutes. Next, poke a meat thermometer into the middle of the thickest part of the meat (not touching a bone), and raise the grill temp up to 325 degrees indirect heat. Cook until the thermometer reads about 135 to 140 for medium rare, about 1 hour. Remove the roast from the grill, tent loosely with foil, and let it rest for about 10 minutes before slicing and serving. Mmm, mmm! Great tasting vittles!

BASKET BUCK BURRITOS

2 pounds deer steak

1 jar salsa

1 can black beans

1 can Mexican-style corn, drained

1 (8-ounce) package cream cheese, cubed

8 (12-inch) flour tortillas, warmed

1 (8-ounce) package shredded Mexican cheese blend

Place the deer steaks into the bottom of a slow cooker; cover with the salsa. Discard half of the liquid from the black beans, then pour the beans into the slow cooker along with the Mexican-style corn. Set the slow cooker on low, and cook for about 8 hours, until the deer meat pulls apart easily with a fork. Break the meat into bite-size pieces, then stir in the cream cheese cubes until melted. Place a tortilla onto your work surface, then spoon some of the filling halfway between the bottom edge and the center of the tortilla. Flatten the filling into a rectangular shape with the back of a spoon. Sprinkle some of the Mexican cheese blend over the filling. Fold the bottom of the tortilla snugly over the filling, then fold in the left and right edges. Roll the burrito up to the top edge, forming a tight cylinder. Repeat with the remaining ingredients.

TIPS FOR CAST IRON SKILLETS

Lots of people ask me how to season and clean a cast iron skillet. It's a great question, so here's my answer: Follow my tips, and you will always have great tasting game vittles! After all, I didn't go through all this work just to have one of my tasty recipes turn out bad because someone didn't do their job of cleaning or seasoning their Dutch oven correctly.

What You'll Need

- Dish soap
- Sponge or stiff brush
- Clean, dry cloths, or paper towels
- Vegetable oil or shortening (or other oil of your choice)
- Aluminum foil

Steps for Cleaning and Seasoning

1. *Get ready.* Gather your supplies, and then preheat oven to 350 degrees.

2. *Wash the skillet.* Wash the skillet with warm, soapy water and a sponge or stiff brush. Cast iron should not normally be washed with soap, but it's fine here since the pan is about to be seasoned.

3. *Rinse and dry.* Rinse and thoroughly dry the skillet with a clean, dry cloth or paper towels.

4. *Add oil.* Pour a little vegetable oil or melted shortening into the skillet. A tablespoon or two is plenty. Vegetable oil and shortening are the most commonly recommended oils for seasoning, but I have found you can use any oil you choose.

5. *Rub.* Use a clean cloth or paper towel to rub the coat around the entire skillet.

6. *Flip the skillet over.* Don't forget the outside—and bottom—of the skillet. You want a thin coat of oil around the entire piece.

7. *Bake the skillet.* Place the skillet upside down on the oven's center rack. Place a sheet of aluminum foil below the rack to catch any drips. Bake for an hour.

8. *Let the skillet cool.* Turn off the heat, and allow the skillet to cool completely before removing from oven. Once it's cooled down, you're good to go!

A seasoned skillet is smooth, shiny, and nonstick. You'll know it's time to re-season if food sticks to the surface or if the skillet appears dull or rusted.

BUBBA'S LAZY HUNTER CHOPS

2 pounds deer chops

1 cup ketchup

½ cup water

1 medium onion, chopped

½ cup packed brown sugar

1 (1-ounce) envelope dry onion soup mix

Thinly slice the deer chops, and brown them in a heavy skillet over medium-high heat. Transfer the meat to a slow cooker. Mix in the ketchup, water, onion, brown sugar, and dry onion soup mix. Cook on low for 8 hours or until tender. Check for seasonings, and serve with your favorite veggies or side.

DEER HUNTER'S TREAT

½ pound deer tenderloin

3 tablespoons zesty Italian dressing

12 slices thick-cut bacon

¼ cup cream cheese

12 slices pickled jalapeño peppers

½ teaspoon seasoned salt (or to taste)

Cut the deer tenderloin into 12 strips lengthwise. Toss with Italian dressing and marinate for 1 hour in the refrigerator. Preheat a grill for medium heat. To assemble the deer wraps, lay a strip of deer on top of a strip of bacon. Place a teaspoon of cream cheese at one end, and top with a slice of jalapeño. Roll up and secure with a skewer. Repeat with remaining ingredients. Season the wraps with desired amount of seasoned salt. Grill for 10 minutes, then turn over, and continue cooking until the bacon is crisp.

City Slicker Hunting

A city slicker was visiting the country and wanted to go hunting.
The Farmer lent the boy his gun, telling him not to kill any farm animals.
The city boy headed off and soon after saw a goat.
He managed to creep into range and finally shot it.
Not knowing anything about animals, the boy didn't know what he'd killed,
so he ran to the farmhouse and described his kill to the Farmer.
"It had two saggy boobs, a beard, a hard head, and it stank like hell!" said the
boy. "Oh, heck!" said the Farmer. "You've shot the wife!"

JEFF AND LINDA'S CANNED DEER MEAT

1 pound lean deer meat, cubed	1 teaspoon minced garlic
1 teaspoon salt	4 slices onion
¼ teaspoon ground black pepper	1 tablespoon minced green bell pepper

Place the venison into a large bowl. Sprinkle with salt, pepper, and garlic; toss to combine. Place venison into a canning jar, along with onions and bell peppers. Jar should be filled to within ½ inch of the top. Wipe rim with a clean, damp cloth, and seal with the lid and ring. Place jar into a pressure canner filled with water according to manufacturer's directions. Affix lid, and bring to a boil with the pressure valve open. Boil for 5 minutes before closing the pressure valve. Bring to a pressure of 10 PSI, then reduce heat in order to maintain this pressure. Process for 75 minutes, watching gauge closely so the pressure stays at 10 PSI. After 75 minutes, turn off heat, and allow the canner to cool until the gauge reads 0 PSI. Once the pressure has subsided and the canner is safe to open, remove the jar to cool on a rack. The jar will seal with a pop as it cools. This is a GREAT tasting deer recipe!

Hunter's Wife

I woke up on Saturday morning, ready to go bag the first deer of the season. I walked down to the kitchen to get a cup of coffee, and to my surprise, I saw Becky, just sitting there, fully dressed in camouflage.

"What are you up to?" I asked.

Becky smiled. "I'm going hunting with you!"

I had my reservations, but, reluctantly, I decided to take her along. And so we arrived at the hunting site.

I set Becky up safely in the tree stand, and I told her, "If you see a deer, take careful aim on it, and I'll come running back as soon as I hear the shot."

I walked away with a smile on my face, knowing Becky couldn't hit an elephant—much less a deer. But not 10 minutes passed when I was startled to hear a flurry of gunshots. I sprinted back.

As I got closer to Becky's stand, I heard her screaming, "Get away from my deer!" Confused, I ran even faster.

And again, I heard her yell, "Get away from my deer!" Followed by another volley of gunfire.

When I finally made it back to Becky, I was surprised to see a cowboy, with his hands high in the air.

The cowboy, obviously distraught, said, "Okay, lady, okay! You can have your deer! Just let me get my saddle off it!"

FARMLAND FRIED DEER STEAKS

1 egg
2 cups whole milk, divided
2 tablespoons hot pepper sauce
2 pounds ½-inch-thick deer steaks
½ cup cornmeal
½ cup seasoned bread crumbs

1 teaspoon cornstarch
1 teaspoon baking soda
1 teaspoon ground black pepper
1 teaspoon garlic salt
1 cup vegetable oil for frying
1 onion, sliced

Beat the egg in a bowl, then whisk in 1 cup of the milk and hot pepper sauce. Pound the deer steaks with a meat mallet until they are ¼ inch thick, and place into the milk mixture. Stir together the cornmeal, bread crumbs, cornstarch, baking soda, black pepper, and garlic salt in a shallow dish. Remove the deer steaks from the milk mixture one at a time, allowing the excess to run off, and press into the bread crumb mixture; set aside. Reserve the remaining bread crumb mixture. Heat the oil in a large skillet over medium heat. Place as many breaded deer steaks into the pan as will fit without overlapping. Cook until the deer is golden brown, about 3 minutes per side. Remove to drain on a paper-towel-lined plate, and keep warm. Repeat with remaining deer. Once the deer has finished cooking, stir the onions into the hot oil, and cook until dark brown, about 5 minutes. Pour off and discard the oil, transfer the onions to a plate, and set aside. Stir the reserved bread crumb mixture into the hot skillet, and cook for a few seconds until it begins to toast. Stir in the remaining cup of milk, and simmer until the milk has thickened, about 5 minutes. Pour the gravy over the deer steaks, and top with the caramelized onions to serve. This is one of my favorite meals!

Whoops

One time at moose camp, Bubba and I were both awake in the middle of the night.

"Look at those stars... What splendor!" I said.

"Yeah," said Bubba, "but what do you think happened to our tent?"

COWHAND DEER AND BISCUITS

BISCUITS:

1 cup self-rising flour

½ tablespoon sugar

2 tablespoons butter, melted

¾ cup milk

DEER:

2 tablespoons butter

1 pound boneless deer steak, cubed

Salt to taste

Ground black pepper to taste

½ cup chicken broth

1 cup milk

1 tablespoon maple syrup

¼ cup all-purpose flour

Preheat oven to 450 degrees. Grease a baking sheet. To make biscuits, mix the self-rising flour and sugar together in a bowl, and stir in the melted butter and ¾ cup milk. Knead the dough very lightly, 5 to 7 times, until it barely hangs together, and roll out to ½-inch thickness on a floured surface. Cut biscuits with a biscuit cutter or the rim of a glass dipped in flour. Bake for 12 to 14 minutes, until the biscuits are golden brown. Melt 2 tablespoons of butter in a large skillet over medium heat, and place the deer meat into the hot butter. Sprinkle the meat with salt and pepper, and pan-fry until golden brown, about 5 minutes. Transfer the meat to a platter. Pour the chicken broth into the skillet, and bring to a boil while scraping the browned bits off the bottom of the skillet with a wooden spoon. Stir in 1 cup of milk and the maple syrup, and whisk in all-purpose flour until smooth. Bring the gravy back to a simmer, add salt and pepper to taste, and allow to thicken, whisking to avoid lumps. Return the deer meat to the gravy, and simmer until the gravy is thick, 5 to 10 minutes. Serve over biscuits.

PLATTEVILLE-STYLE DEER ROAST VITTLES

1 egg

1/3 cup light cream

1 cup fine bread crumbs

1 cup grated Parmesan cheese

1/4 cup minced fresh parsley

2 pounds boneless deer roast

Salt to taste

Ground black pepper to taste

1/4 cup all-purpose flour for dredging

1/4 cup butter

1 clove garlic, minced

1/2 cup dry sherry

1/2 cup venison broth (or beef broth or water)

Preheat oven to 375 degrees. Stir together the egg and cream, and set aside. Combine the bread crumbs, Parmesan, and parsley in a large bowl; set aside. Slice deer roast into serving-size portions, 3/8-inch thick. Pound with a meat mallet to about 1/4-inch thickness. Season to taste with salt and pepper, then dredge in flour, shaking off the excess. Dip the deer into the eggs, then press into the bread crumbs. Melt butter in an oven-safe frying pan with lid. Cook garlic until fragrant, then add the breaded deer, and cook on both sides until browned. Pour in sherry and deer broth. Bring to a simmer, cover, then transfer to the oven, and bake until the deer is tender, about 45 minutes. Check for seasonings, and serve.

MIDWEST CORNED DEER MEAT

2 cups water for boiling

6 tablespoons sugar-based curing salt

1/2 cup brown sugar

5 teaspoons pickling spice

1 tablespoon garlic powder

6 cups cold water for brining

5 pounds boneless shoulder deer roast

Bring 2 cups of water to a boil in a saucepan over high heat. Stir in the curing salt, brown sugar, pickling spice, and garlic powder; stir until dissolved, then remove from the heat. Pour 6 cups of cold water into a 2-gallon container, and stir in the spice mixture. Place the boneless deer meat into the brine, cover, and refrigerate. Leave the venison in the refrigerator to brine for 5 days, turning the meat over every day. To cook, rinse the meat well, place into a large pot, and cover with water. Bring to a boil, then reduce heat to medium-low, cover, and simmer for 6 hours. Remove the deer from the pot, and allow to rest for about 45 minutes before slicing. This is a great way to cook an old buck and make it tender with outstanding flavor.

GAVIN AND MASON'S "NUGIN AND BUBBA'S" GRANDPA'S BOYS DEER RIBS

1 cup apple cider vinegar
1 dark ale beer
4 celery ribs, chopped
4 carrots, chopped
3 red bell peppers, chopped
1 clove garlic, peeled

1 onion, chopped
6 to 8 pounds deer ribs
2 tablespoons Cajun seasoning
Salt to taste
Ground black pepper to taste

Preheat oven to 200 degrees. Pour vinegar and beer into a large roasting pan. Add the celery, carrots, peppers, garlic, and onion. Rub the deer ribs with Cajun seasoning, salt, and pepper to taste. Place ribs in roasting pan, and cover with a tight-fitting lid or aluminum foil. Bake in oven for about 20 hours or until the rib meat is falling off the bone and very tender.

©2018 Dan Roberts

"Why do I always see you guys when it's NOT deer hunting season?"

"HEY CRACK THAT WINDOW OPEN!" DEER HUNTER BEANS

DEER:

1 large deer roast

1 liter ginger ale

1 large can chicken stock

1 teaspoon ground cumin

½ teaspoon fresh cracked black pepper

¼ teaspoon crushed red pepper flakes

BEAN MIXTURE:

1 can pork and beans

1 can black beans, drained and rinsed

1 can red kidney beans, drained and rinsed

1 can baked beans

1 can diced tomatoes

1 large green bell pepper, coarsely chopped

1 large Vidalia onion, coarsely chopped

1 bottle Carolina-style barbecue sauce

¹/₃ cup brown sugar

¼ cup molasses

1 teaspoon ground cumin

¼ teaspoon crushed red pepper flakes (or to taste)

2 tablespoons chili powder

Hot pepper sauce to taste

Salt to taste

Ground black pepper to taste

6 bacon slices

Place deer roast, ginger ale, chicken stock, 1 teaspoon cumin, pepper, and ¼ teaspoon red pepper flakes into a slow cooker. Cover, and cook on low until the deer is tender enough to be pulled apart with a fork, about 10 hours. Drain meat, and shred. Preheat oven to 350 degrees. Place shredded deer into a large mixing bowl, and mix with pork and beans, black beans, kidney beans, baked beans, tomatoes, green pepper, and onion. Pour in barbecue sauce, brown sugar, and molasses. Season with cumin, red pepper flakes, chili powder, hot pepper sauce, salt, and pepper. Mix until well combined, then pour into a deep 9- by 13-inch glass baking dish. Place bacon strips in a single layer over top. Bake for 30 to 40 minutes until bacon has cooked and begins to crisp. Check deer and beans for flavor, and serve. This is a great meal during cold-weather deer hunting.

ALPHA BUCK BIG DADDY DEER RIBS
WITH WHISKEY

DEER:

2 large slabs of ribs from large harvest deer
(or 4 slabs if you are using small deer)
Salt to taste

Coarsely ground black pepper to taste
1 tablespoon ground red chili pepper

SAUCE:

2¼ tablespoons vegetable oil
½ cup minced onion
1½ cups water
½ cup tomato paste
½ cup white vinegar
½ cup brown sugar
2½ tablespoons honey
2 tablespoons Worcestershire sauce
2 teaspoons salt

¼ teaspoon coarsely ground black pepper
1¼ teaspoons liquid smoke flavoring
2 teaspoons whiskey
2 teaspoons garlic powder
¼ teaspoon paprika
½ teaspoon onion powder
1 tablespoon dark molasses
½ tablespoon ground red chili pepper

Preheat oven to 300 degrees. Cut each rack of deer ribs in half, so that you have 4 half racks. Sprinkle salt and pepper (more pepper than salt), and 1 tablespoon chili pepper over deer meat. Wrap each half rack in aluminum foil. Bake for 2½ hours. Meanwhile, heat oil in a medium saucepan over medium heat. Cook and stir the onions in oil for 5 minutes. Stir in water, tomato paste, vinegar, brown sugar, honey, and Worcestershire sauce. Season with 2 teaspoons salt, ¼ teaspoon black pepper, liquid smoke, whiskey, garlic powder, paprika, onion powder, dark molasses, and ½ tablespoon ground chili pepper. Bring mixture to a boil, then reduce heat. Simmer for 1¼ hours, uncovered, or until sauce thickens. Remove from heat, and set sauce aside. Preheat an outdoor grill for high heat. Remove the deer ribs from the oven, and let stand 10 minutes. Remove the racks from the foil, and place on the grill. Grill the deer ribs for 3 to 4 minutes on each side. Brush sauce on the deer ribs while they're grilling, just before you serve them. These are mouth-watering vittles!

CROCKPOT VENISON RIBS (EASY AND TASTY)

4 pounds deer ribs

Salt to taste

Ground black pepper to taste

2 cups ketchup

1 cup chili sauce

½ cup packed brown sugar

4 tablespoons vinegar

2 teaspoons dried oregano

2 teaspoons Worcestershire sauce

1 dash hot sauce

Preheat oven to 400 degrees. Season deer ribs with salt and pepper. Place in a shallow baking pan. Brown in oven for 15 minutes. Turn over and brown for another 15 minutes; drain fat. In a medium bowl, mix together the ketchup, chili sauce, brown sugar, vinegar, oregano, Worcestershire sauce, and hot sauce, along with salt and pepper. Place the deer ribs in a slow cooker. Pour sauce over ribs, and turn to coat. Cover, and cook on low for about 8 hours, or until the deer ribs are tender.

WILD GAME FEED DEER MEAT WITH TATERS CASSEROLE

1 pound deer burger

1 (10.75-ounce) can condensed cream of mushroom soup

½ cup chopped onion

¾ cup milk

Salt to taste

Freshly ground black pepper to taste

3 cups peeled and thinly sliced potatoes

cup shredded cheddar cheese

Preheat oven to 350 degrees. In a medium skillet over medium heat, brown the deer burger; drain any fat. In a medium mixing bowl, combine cream of mushroom soup, onion, milk, and salt and pepper to taste. Alternately layer the potatoes, soup mixture, and deer meat in an 11- by 7-inch (2-quart) baking dish. Bake in oven for 1 to 1½ hours or until potatoes are tender. Top with cheddar cheese, and continue baking until cheese is melted. Check for seasonings, and serve.

DUTCH OVEN DEER HEART STEW

1 deer heart, rinsed and cubed

2 tablespoons all-purpose flour

2 tablespoons vegetable oil

1 large onion, peeled and sliced

1 cup water

2 teaspoons salt

½ teaspoon seasoned salt

Before starting, make sure your deer heart is free of shot—I say this because most of my shots are to the heart. Dredge the deer heart in flour until coated. Heat the oil in a Dutch oven over medium-high heat. Fry the pieces of heart until browned. Stir in onions and water. Sprinkle with salt and seasoned salt. Cover, reduce heat to low, and simmer for 2 to 3 hours or until the deer meat is very tender. Serve over noodles or mashed potatoes.

MY DUTCH OVEN DEER STEAK

1 large deer steak

2 tablespoons olive oil

1 pinch salt

¼ cup all-purpose flour (or as needed)

¾ cup beef stock

1 can artichoke hearts, chopped and with juice reserved

½ cup roasted red peppers, drained and chopped

½ can chopped green chilis

3 tablespoons prepared horseradish

2 teaspoons capers

Preheat oven to 400 degrees. Pound the deer steak with a meat mallet to tenderize; flip steak, and repeat on other side. Cut deer steak into 6 to 8 pieces. Heat olive oil in an oven-safe Dutch oven over medium heat. Season both sides of steak pieces with salt; coat with a thin layer of flour. Cook the deer steak in the hot oil until browned, about 2 minutes per side. Remove steak from Dutch oven. Pour beef stock and ¼ cup reserved artichoke juice into the Dutch oven, scraping any brown bits of food from the bottom. Mix artichokes, red peppers, green chilis, horseradish, and capers into broth mixture; bring to a boil. Return venison to broth mixture in Dutch oven, and cover. Place Dutch oven in the oven, and bake until meat is tender, 45 to 60 minutes. Allow steak to cool in Dutch oven for 15 minutes before serving.

JAIME MARTINEZ MUSCATINE VENISON SOUP

1 pound deer roast, chopped

1 tomato, quartered

2 potatoes, cubed

1 onion, chopped

3 carrots, chopped

½ medium head cabbage, chopped

4 cloves garlic, minced

5 teaspoons chopped fresh cilantro,

(plus another teaspoon for garnish)

1 tablespoon salt

¼ teaspoon ground cumin

2 fluid ounces fresh lime juice

In a large pot over low heat, combine the deer, tomato, potatoes, onion, carrots, cabbage, garlic, cilantro, salt, and cumin. Add water to cover, and stir well. Cover, and simmer for 2 hours. Remove lid, stir, and simmer for another hour with lid off. Serve hot. Just before eating, squeeze in fresh lime juice to taste, and sprinkle with remaining cilantro. Check for seasonings, and serve. This is a great spicy soup!

VENISON HEART BRAISED IN WINE

1 deer heart

¼ cup all-purpose flour

Salt to taste

Ground black pepper to taste

3 tablespoons butter

1 onion, chopped

2 carrots, chopped

2 potatoes, chopped

2 teaspoons dried thyme

1 cup beef broth

½ cup red wine

Wash the deer heart, and remove any fat and arteries. Slice the heart in half, then slice it into ½-inch-thick slices. Dredge slices in flour, and season them with salt and pepper. Heat the butter in a large sauté pan over medium-high heat. Add the deer heart slices, and cook for 30 to 45 seconds per side. Stir in the onion, carrots, potatoes, thyme, beef broth, and wine. Reduce heat to low, cover, and simmer for 1 hour. Check for seasonings, and serve.

HUNT SHACK VENISON

4 pounds venison steaks

1½ teaspoons seasoned salt, divided

1 cup all-purpose flour

4 tablespoons vegetable oil

½ teaspoon ground cumin

½ cup sliced onions

2 beef bouillon cubes

½ teaspoon dried Mexican oregano

1 bay leaf

2 dried red chili peppers, whole but with the stems removed

2 cups water

Lightly season the venison steaks with ½ teaspoon of seasoned salt. Cut the steaks into bite-sized pieces. Mix the flour with remaining 1 teaspoon of seasoned salt; reserve 1 tablespoon of the flour mixture, and set aside. Toss the cubed meat in the seasoned flour. Heat the oil in the pressure cooker or a skillet over medium-high heat. Add the meat cubes in batches, and cook until richly browned on all sides. Remove the meat, and set aside. Reduce the heat to medium, and stir the reserved tablespoon of seasoned flour and the ground cumin into the pan drippings. Cook, stirring, until the flour has lost its raw smell and is lightly browned, about 5 minutes. Add the sliced onions, and cook, still stirring often, until the onions have softened, about 5 minutes. Return the meat to the pan, along with the beef bouillon cubes, Mexican oregano, bay leaf, and chili peppers. Pour in the water, and seal the pressure cooker, turning the heat up to high. Bring the pressure up to high, and reduce the heat to maintain the pressure. Cook at high pressure for 15 minutes. Turn off the heat, and let the pressure drop naturally. Remove the lid. Take out the chili peppers and bay leaf; squeeze the pulp from the peppers, returning the pulp to the pan and discarding the skins and the bay leaf. Taste, and adjust the seasonings.

CROSSBOW APPLE SLOW-COOKED VENISON

1 tablespoon olive oil

3 pounds boneless venison roast

1 large apple, cored and quartered

2 small onions, sliced

4 cloves garlic, crushed

1 cup boiling water

1 cube beef bouillon

Spread the olive oil on the inside of a slow cooker. Place the venison roast inside, and cover with apple, onions, and garlic. Turn to low, and cook until the roast is tender, about 8 hours. When the roast has cooked, remove it from the slow cooker, and place onto a serving platter. Discard the apple. Stir the water and bouillon into the slow cooker until the bouillon has dissolved. Serve this as a sauce with the roast.

OLD JEB TUCKER'S DEER LOINS WITH BACON, MAN!

6 thick slices bacon

2 large venison tenderloin roasts

2 teaspoons olive oil, divided

¼ teaspoon onion powder, divided

Seasoned salt to taste

Ground black pepper to taste

2 tablespoons butter

1 package sliced cremini mushrooms

2 cloves garlic, chopped

1 tablespoon chopped green onion

½ cup heavy whipping cream

Preheat oven to 375 degrees. Place bacon on a slotted baking pan. Bake bacon in oven until partially cooked but still flexible, 6 to 8 minutes. Brush venison tenderloins with olive oil, and season with onion powder, salt, and black pepper. Place tenderloin roasts side by side, and wrap them together in strips of partially cooked bacon. Place into a roasting pan. Roast until bacon is browned and an instant-read meat thermometer inserted into the thickest part of a tenderloin reads at least 160 degrees, about 1 hour. Heat butter in a saucepan over medium heat; cook mushrooms and garlic in hot butter while stirring until mushrooms are soft, 8 to 10 minutes. Stir green onion into mushroom mixture; pour in cream. Cook, again stirring often, until sauce is heated through. Serve sauce with tenderloins.

CRANDALL'S BUCK IN THE BRUSH DEER BACKSTRAPS

1 large deer backstrap, cut into ¼-inch-thick slices

2½ cups milk, divided

2 tablespoons hot pepper sauce

Oil for frying

2 eggs

3 cups all-purpose flour

2 tablespoons garlic salt

1 tablespoon ground black pepper

Place the venison slices into a shallow bowl, and pour in 2 cups of the milk and hot sauce. Stir to coat, then cover, and marinate for 1 hour. Heat the vegetable oil in an electric skillet to 325 degrees. In a shallow bowl, whisk together the eggs and remaining ½ cup of milk. In a separate bowl, stir together the flour, garlic salt, and pepper. Dip the venison slices into the flour, then into the egg and milk, then back into the flour. Shake off excess flour. Fry in the hot oil until lightly browned on each side, about 4 minutes. Remove with tongs, and drain lightly on paper towels before serving.

OLD COUNTRY DEER RIBS SOUP

MEATBALLS:

1 cup ground chicken liver

1 cup dried bread crumbs

3 tablespoons all-purpose flour

2 eggs

¼ tablespoon chopped fresh parsley

1 teaspoon salt

⅛ teaspoon dried marjoram

⅛ teaspoon ground mace

1 clove garlic, minced

SOUP MIXTURE:

2 pounds deer ribs

2 onions, thinly sliced

3 stalks chopped celery, with leaves

4 teaspoons salt

¾ teaspoon ground black pepper

8 cups water

2 carrots, halved

3 tomatoes, chopped

4 sprigs fresh parsley

Combine liver, bread crumbs, flour, eggs, parsley, 1 teaspoon salt, marjoram, mace, and garlic. Mix thoroughly, and set aside. Let meatball mixture stand. Rinse the deer ribs, and place in a large stockpot. Add onions, celery, 4 teaspoons salt, pepper, water, carrots, tomatoes, and parsley. Cover, and bring to a boil. Skim surface of soup. Simmer for 1½ hours, or until deer meat is tender. Remove meat, bones, and carrots from soup. Cut deer rib meat and carrots into bite-size pieces; return to soup. Bring to a boil. Shape meatball mixture into balls the size of golf balls; drop into soup. Cover, and cook for 10 minutes. This recipe will take some time to prepare, but the flavor is outstanding. It's a popular meal that I'm often asked to cook.

Cousin Rick's Deer Camp Quickies

Q: Who did Bambi invite to his birthday party?

A: His nearest and deer-est friends.

Q: What's the cheapest kind of meat?

A: Deer balls. They're under a buck!

WOOLLIES DEER ROAST & COUNTY FAIR-AWARDED GRAVY

1 large boneless deer roast, thinly sliced
across the grain
1 tablespoon minced garlic
1 tablespoon grill seasoning

1 teaspoon chili powder
2 cups beef broth
¼ cup butter
¼ cup flour

Preheat oven to 350 degrees. Season the deer with garlic, grill seasoning, and chili powder. Place into a casserole dish, and pour in the beef broth. Cover the dish with a lid, and bake in oven until the deer is tender, about 1 hour. Meanwhile, melt the butter in a saucepan over medium heat. Once the butter begins to bubble, whisk in the flour. Cook while whisking constantly until the flour turns a golden yellow and the bubbling slows, about 10 minutes. When the deer has finished cooking, whisk 1½ cups of the broth from the deer roast into the flour roux, and simmer for 15 minutes, whisking frequently. Add the deer to the gravy, and serve.

"ICE IN MY BOOTS" STEW

2 pounds venison stew meat
2 tablespoons vegetable oil
3 onions, chopped
2 cloves garlic, minced
1 tablespoon Worcestershire sauce
1 bay leaf
½ teaspoon dried thyme

1 tablespoon salt
3 cups beef stock
8 small potatoes, peeled and quartered
1 pound parsnips, chopped
¼ cup all-purpose flour
¼ cup water

In a large Dutch oven or pot, deeply brown the deer meat in oil. Stir in onions, garlic, Worcestershire sauce, bay leaf, thyme, salt, and beef stock. Simmer, covered, for 1½ to 2 hours, or until meat is tender. Stir in potatoes and parsnips; cook until tender. Combine flour and water. Stir into the stew. Remove bay leaf before serving.

HIGH-POWERED GRILLED VENISON

1 big deer roast
1½ cups water
1 cup chicken broth
½ cup olive oil
3 tablespoons butter
3 cloves garlic, minced
1 teaspoon hot sauce
1 tablespoon distilled white vinegar

¼ cup chopped fresh parsley
3 leaves fresh basil, chopped
2 tablespoons fresh rosemary
1 teaspoon ground cumin
½ teaspoon paprika
Seasoned salt to taste
Ground black pepper to taste

Slice deer roast into 1-inch-thick steaks. In a saucepan, combine water, chicken broth, olive oil, butter, garlic, and hot sauce; bring to a boil. Reduce heat, and stir in vinegar. Season with parsley, basil, rosemary, cumin, paprika, salt, and pepper. Simmer for 20 minutes, stirring regularly. Allow to cool. Pour cooled sauce over deer steaks, and marinate in the refrigerator for at least 4 hours, turning regularly. Preheat an outdoor grill for high heat, and lightly oil grate. Take steaks out of marinade, reserving marinade. Grill steaks for 7 to 8 minutes per side or to desired doneness. Turn them regularly, making sure you don't overcook. Mop steaks with reserved marinade while cooking. Check for seasonings, and serve!

NAUVOO-STYLE DEER TENDERLOIN

1 whole deer tenderloin
½ cup teriyaki sauce
½ cup Nauvoo grape wine
(or substitute wine of your choice)
2 cloves garlic, chopped

4 ounces Nauvoo blue cheese, crumbled
(or substitute your favorite blue cheese)
1/3 cup mayonnaise
2/3 cup sour cream
2 teaspoons Worcestershire sauce

Place the deer loin in a shallow dish. Combine teriyaki sauce, wine, and garlic; pour over deer meat. Allow the deer loin to marinate in refrigerator for 30 minutes. Preheat oven to 450 degrees. Place the deer tenderloin on broiler pan, and cook in oven for 15 minutes. Reduce heat to 375 degrees, and cook for 30 to 40 more minutes, or to desired doneness. Allow to set for 10 minutes before slicing. In a saucepan over low heat, combine the Nauvoo blue cheese, mayonnaise, sour cream, and Worcestershire sauce. Stir until smooth; serve over sliced deer tenderloin.

BIG BUCK GRILLED BACKSTRAP

2 pounds venison backstrap, cut into 2-inch chunks

1 quart apple cider

3 cups South Carolina–style barbecue sauce (or substitute your favorite barbecue sauce)

2 pounds thick sliced bacon

Place chunks of venison into a shallow baking dish, and add enough of the apple cider to submerge it. Cover, and refrigerate for 2 hours. Remove, and pat dry. Discard apple cider, and return venison to the dish. Pour barbecue sauce over the chunks, cover again, and refrigerate for 4 to 8 hours. Preheat an outdoor charcoal grill for high heat. Remove the deer meat from the refrigerator, and let stand for 30 minutes. Wrap each chunk of venison in a slice of bacon, and secure with toothpicks. Brush the grill grate with olive oil when hot, and place venison pieces on the grill. Grill, turning occasionally, until the bacon becomes dark brown. Check for seasonings, and serve.

DEER & DUMPLINGS SOUP

2 tablespoons butter

1 cup chopped onion

1 clove garlic, chopped

3 carrots, chopped

2 cups chopped celery

2 cans condensed beef broth

2 cups red wine

2 cups tomato juice

2 cups diced cooked deer steak or roast

Salt to taste

Ground black pepper to taste

2 tablespoons margarine (or butter), softened

2 eggs

6 tablespoons all-purpose flour

¼ teaspoon salt

In a large pot, using 2 tablespoons of butter, sauté onion, garlic, carrots, and celery until soft, about 5 to 6 minutes. Stir in broth, wine, tomato juice, and deer meat. Simmer covered for 15 to 20 minutes, or until vegetables are tender. Season to taste with salt and pepper. In a bowl, mix 2 tablespoons margarine, eggs, flour, and salt until smooth. Drop mixture into soup by small teaspoonfuls. Cover, and simmer for 10 minutes. Check for seasonings, and serve with fresh rye bread.

SEASONED MULE DEER VITTLES

2 pounds mule deer venison
½ cup Worcestershire sauce
1 can beer
1½ cups all-purpose flour

1 tablespoon seasoned salt
1 tablespoon garlic powder
Vegetable oil for frying

Pound the deer meat flat, and cut into 1-inch strips; place in a large bowl. Pour in Worcestershire sauce and beer. Cover, and refrigerate for 3 hours or more. In a shallow bowl, combine flour, seasoned salt, and garlic powder. Shake soaked meat through the flour mixture. Heat oil in a large, heavy skillet or Dutch oven, and fry meat until golden brown. This is a great tasting recipe that is quick to do and takes all that game taste out of mule deer.

CABIN ROAST AND NOODLES

4 tablespoons olive oil
2 pounds deer stew meat
1 teaspoon seasoned salt
1 teaspoon ground black pepper
1 teaspoon garlic powder

1 teaspoon onion powder
1 tablespoon all-purpose flour
1 cup beef stock
1 can condensed cream of mushroom soup
1 (16-ounce) package uncooked egg noodles

Heat the olive oil in a large cast iron skillet over high heat. Toss the cubed deer meat with seasoned salt, pepper, garlic powder, and onion powder. Cook the deer meat in the hot oil until browned on all sides. After meat is browned, remove from the iron skillet and place into a slow cooker, leaving the remaining oil in the skillet. Reduce skillet's heat to medium-low, and stir the flour into the remaining olive oil. Simmer and stir until the flour has turned golden brown. Stir in the stock, and bring to a simmer, then pour into the slow cooker along with the cream of mushroom soup. Cover, and cook on low for 6 to 8 hours or until the deer meat is tender. Bring a large pot of lightly salted water to a boil. Add the egg noodles, and cook until tender; drain. Spoon the meat over the egg noodles, check again for seasonings, and serve hot.

EARLY DAYS TENDER DEER

2 pounds venison steaks
1½ teaspoons seasoned salt, divided
1 cup all-purpose flour
4 tablespoons vegetable oil
½ teaspoon ground cumin
½ cup sliced onions

2 beef bouillon cubes
½ teaspoon dried oregano
1 bay leaf
2 dried red chili peppers
2 cups water

Lightly season the venison steaks with ½ teaspoon of seasoned salt. Cut the steaks into chunks. Mix the flour with remaining 1 teaspoon of seasoned salt; reserve 1 tablespoon of the flour mixture, and set aside. Toss the cubed deer meat in the seasoned flour. Heat the oil in the pressure cooker over high heat. Add the deer cubes in batches, and cook until browned on all sides. Remove the meat, and set aside. Reduce the heat to medium, and stir the reserved tablespoon of seasoned flour and the ground cumin into the pan drippings. Cook and stir until the flour is lightly browned. Add the sliced onions, and cook, stirring often, until the onions have softened. Return the deer meat to the pan, along with the beef bouillon cubes, oregano, bay leaf, and chili peppers. Pour in the water, and seal the pressure cooker, turning the heat up to high. Bring the pressure up to high and then reduce the heat to maintain the pressure. Cook at high pressure for about 20 minutes. Turn off the heat, and let the pressure drop. Remove the lid. Take out the chili peppers and bay leaf. Check again for seasonings, and serve. This is a very tender and great tasting meal!

FUN AT CAMP JERKY

¾ cup Worcestershire sauce
¼ cup soy sauce
1 tablespoon liquid smoke flavoring
1 tablespoon fresh lemon juice
3 tablespoons teriyaki sauce
1 tablespoon ketchup

1 teaspoon hot pepper sauce (or to taste)
1 tablespoon garlic powder
1 teaspoon onion powder
1 teaspoon black pepper
1-pound venison, cut into 1- by ¼-inch strips

Stir together Worcestershire sauce, soy sauce, liquid smoke, lemon juice, teriyaki sauce, ketchup, and hot pepper sauce in a bowl. Season with garlic powder, onion powder, and pepper. Mix in the sliced venison until completely coated. Cover tightly, and marinate at least 8 hours in the refrigerator. Prepare jerky in a food dehydrator according to manufacturer's directions, or dry on racks in the oven at 150 degrees until the jerky has dried and will snap when bent, 10 to 12 hours.

THE BLACK FAMILY'S VENISON BLOOD SAUSAGE

3 pounds venison roast, cut into 2-inch cubes

8 ounces pork back fat, cut into 1-inch cubes

1 teaspoon black peppercorns

½ teaspoon coriander seeds

2 whole cloves

2 bay leaves

5 tablespoons butter

1 onion, diced

1½ tablespoons salt

2 tart apples, peeled and diced

2 ounces cognac

1 handful fresh thyme, leaves picked and stems reserved

2 cups cooked wild rice

2 teaspoons paprika

3 cups venison blood

1 hog casing

Poaching bath

4 tablespoons salt

2 bay leaves

1 onion, chopped

1 teaspoon black pepper

Place the venison and the fat in the freezer for 30 minutes. Also, place the meat mincer in the freezer, as this will make mincing easier. Toast the peppercorns, coriander seeds, cloves, and bay leaves in a dry frying pan over high heat for 1 to 2 minutes. Once fragrant, grind to a powder with a mortar and pestle. Melt the butter in a large iron skillet over medium-high heat. Add the onion and a pinch of the salt, and cook about 2 minutes. Add the apples, stir well, and cook 3 minutes more. Pour in the cognac, and sprinkle over the thyme leaves; stir well, and cook a further minute, then remove from heat and let cool. Pass the partially frozen venison roast and pork back fat mix through the cold meat mincer fitted with a medium plate. Combine the mince with the wild rice, apple mixture, salt, and spice mix. Mix well for at least 3 minutes, using your hands, till the mixture starts to congeal. Cover with cling film, and chill overnight. Place the blood in a food processor, and blend until smooth. Add the blood to the mince mixture along with the back fat. Fold together with a spatula until combined. Soak the casing in cold water for about 30 minutes. Place the wide end of a small sausage stuffing funnel up against the sink tap, and run cold water through the inside of the casing. Using a medium sausage stuffing funnel attachment, thread the casing onto the outside of the tube. Start passing the meat mixture through the funnel, stopping as it just starts to come out the other end. Tie the casing into a knot at the end, then continue passing the meat mixture through the funnel, supporting the sausage with your other hand. Once it reaches the desired length, tie the other end of the casing into a knot, then bring the two ends of the sausage together, and tie into a ring by knotting together the two ends of casing. Repeat until the meat mixture is finished. Place the sausages and the poaching bath ingredients in a large saucepan or stockpot. Add water to cover. Bring the water to just below simmering, about 175 degrees, and hold there for 45 minutes. Remove the sausages from the poaching bath, and place in a large bowl of ice water for a couple of minutes to stop cooking and cool. Enjoy the sausage sliced and served cold or fried till evenly browned. This is a diehard deer hunter's recipe that has been in our family for years. Enjoy!

EASY DEER LOINS FOR WILD GAME COOK-OFFS

3 cups dark brown sugar

2 cups soy sauce

2 pounds venison tenderloins

½ pound bacon

Mix brown sugar and soy sauce together in a bowl. Put deer loin in a cooking tray, and pour brown sugar/soy sauce mixture over loin. Roll tenderloin over in mixture, completely covering it. Let meat marinate in mixture at least 8 hours or overnight in fridge. Remove loin from tray, and place on a slotted baking sheet with a drip pan or aluminum foil below to catch dripping. Save the marinade. Wrap a piece of bacon around the very end of the tenderloin, securing the bacon strip with a toothpick. Repeat this process until the entire loin is wrapped. The tenderloin should be well covered. Drizzle remaining marinade over deer loin. Place on center rack in oven, and bake at 350 degrees for 30 to 40 minutes. You can continue to baste the loin with the marinade throughout the cooking process with either a brush or a turkey baster.

BUBBA'S SECRET BIG BUCK BOLOGNA

1 pound ground venison

1 pound ground pork (sausage)

1 teaspoon black pepper

½ teaspoon onion powder

½ teaspoon garlic powder

2 tablespoons Morton Tender Quick

½ teaspoon mustard seeds

1 teaspoon red pepper

½ teaspoon liquid smoke flavoring

1 cup water

Mix ground venison and pork, and all dry ingredients in a large bowl; cover with the water. Put bowl in refrigerator for 24 hours. Preheat oven to 350 degrees. Form into 2 rolls. Bake uncovered in oven on a cake rack or cookie sheet so grease will drop off while baking, 1 hour to 1 hour, 15 minutes. Take out of oven, and let cool. Cut just like venison bologna.

RASPBERRY VINAIGRETTE VENISON DISH

¾ cup raspberry vinaigrette

2 tablespoons maple syrup

2 tablespoons soy sauce

2 pounds venison, cut into ½-inch strips

2 tablespoons butter

2 tablespoons olive oil

¾ cup water

2 sweet onions, thinly sliced

1 tablespoon minced garlic

Salt to taste

Ground black pepper to taste

2 tablespoons sugar

Whisk together the raspberry vinaigrette, maple syrup, and soy sauce in a large bowl. Stir in the venison until well coated, and set aside. Bring the butter, olive oil, water, onions, and garlic to a boil in a large skillet over medium-high heat. Season with salt and pepper. Cook and stir until the onions have caramelized to a deep, golden brown, 10 to 15 minutes. Once the onions have turned dark golden brown, stir in the sugar, and cook 2 to 3 minutes more. Stir in the venison along with the marinade. Cook and stir until the venison is no longer pink in the center, about 5 minutes. Check for seasonings, and serve.

EASY DEER JERKY

¼ cup soy sauce

¼ cup balsamic vinegar

¼ cup Worcestershire sauce

2 teaspoons liquid smoke flavoring

1½ tablespoons steak seasoning rub

1 medium-size deer roast, thinly sliced along the grain

Combine the soy sauce, balsamic vinegar, Worcestershire sauce, liquid smoke, and steak seasoning in a saucepan, and bring to a boil. Reduce heat to low, and simmer for about 10 minutes. Remove from the heat, and set aside to cool. Pour the marinade into a glass or plastic bowl, and add the deer meat slices. Stir to coat, and then cover and refrigerate for up to 2 days. Turn or stir occasionally to marinate the meat evenly. Preheat the oven to 175 degrees. Arrange the deer strips on a wire rack set over a baking sheet. If you like, you can sprinkle on a little more steak seasoning at this point. Bake meat for 60 to 90 minutes, until dry but still pliable. Store in an airtight container in the refrigerator. I like to top mine with freshly ground pepper to give it a kick.

HUNTER'S DEER DIP

1 (8-ounce) package cream cheese, softened
1 cup shredded white cheddar cheese, divided
½ cup sour cream

1 package brown gravy mix
2 ounces deer jerky, shredded or cut into bite-size
pieces

Preheat oven to 350 degrees. Mix cream cheese, ½ cup of the shredded cheese, sour cream, and gravy in a medium bowl until well blended. Stir in deer jerky. Spoon into a glass pie plate that has been sprayed with nonstick cooking spray. Top with remaining ½ cup cheese. Bake 15 minutes or until heated through. Serve with crusty bread or crackers—and of course, ice-cold brew dogs!

"I'll have that dutch oven lit it a second, Cousin."

WWW.ROBERTSBOOKSANDTOONS.COM

©2016 Dan Roberts

CHAPTER 5

Ground Venison Cooking

I love cooking with deer burger. In fact, I wrote one of the best-selling books about it: *Deer Burger Cookbook*. If you're really good and obey all the hunting laws, I will even autograph it for you! Anyway, here are several of my most-requested and award-winning recipes using ground venison.

BUCK IN RUT BURGERS

6 slices bacon, minced

2 tablespoons olive oil

1 teaspoon minced garlic

2 shallots, minced

2 pounds deer burger

1 tablespoon Worcestershire sauce

1 tablespoon chopped fresh parsley

Salt to taste

Fresh ground white pepper to taste

1 egg, beaten

6 hamburger buns

Cook bacon in a skillet over medium heat until browned and crispy. Pour bacon and grease into a heatproof bowl, and allow to cool. Heat olive oil in skillet, then add garlic and shallots. Cook and stir until softened, about 3 minutes, then add to bacon. Once cool, mix in the deer burger, Worcestershire sauce, parsley, salt, pepper, and egg until evenly combined. Refrigerate for 20 minutes. Preheat an outdoor grill for medium-high heat. Shape the mixture into 6 patties, and grill to desired doneness. Serve on toasted hamburger buns with your favorite toppings.

DEER IN THE BEER CAMP CHILI

¼ cup butter

1 pound deer burger

1 pound cubed venison stew meat

1 pound cubed pork stew meat

1 large onion, chopped

1 fresh jalapeño pepper, seeded and minced

3 tablespoons chili powder

½ teaspoon cayenne pepper

1½ teaspoons ground cumin

2 (14-ounce) cans stewed tomatoes, with juice

1 (15-ounce) can tomato sauce

6 cloves garlic, minced

4 cubes beef bouillon, crumbled

¼ cup Kentucky bourbon

2 (12-fluid ounce) cans pilsner-style beer

2 cups water

Melt the butter in a large pot over medium heat. Cook the deer burger, venison, and pork in the melted butter until completely browned. Add the onion and jalapeño; cook until tender. Season with chili powder, cayenne pepper, and cumin. Stir in the stewed tomatoes (with juice), tomato sauce, garlic, and beef bouillon. Pour the bourbon, beer, and water into the mixture, and stir. Bring the chili to a boil; cover, and reduce heat to medium-low. Simmer about 1 hour, stirring frequently.

OLD BUCK HUNTER–STYLE BACON DEER BURGERS

6 slices hickory-smoked bacon

½ pound ground venison

½ pound lean ground beef

Seasoned salt to taste

Freshly ground black pepper to taste

Dash of stout beer

Dash of Worcestershire sauce

4 hamburger buns

Place the bacon in a large, deep skillet, and cook over medium-high heat, turning occasionally until evenly browned, about 10 minutes. Drain the bacon slices on a paper towel–lined plate. Combine ground venison and ground beef in a bowl. Divide into 4 balls, and flatten into patties. Heat a large skillet over medium heat. Place the burgers in the heated skillet, and sprinkle each burger with salt, black pepper, a dash of beer, and a dash of Worcestershire sauce. Flip the burgers once a brown crust has formed on the bottom, after about 5 to 10 minutes. Sprinkle the cooked side of the burgers with more salt, pepper, beer, and Worcestershire. Cook burgers another 5 to 10 minutes for well done. Top each patty with bacon, and serve on hamburger buns.

TWELVE GAUGE STEW

3 pounds ground venison

2 large onions, diced

2 tablespoons chili powder

6 potatoes, diced

1 pound carrots, diced

3 cups white hominy

3 cans whole peeled tomatoes with liquid, chopped

2 cans chopped green chilis with juice

3 cups beef broth

½ teaspoon salt (or to taste)

½ teaspoon ground black pepper (or to taste)

In a large pot over medium heat, cook deer burger until evenly browned. Stir in onions, and sauté until soft and translucent. Season with chili powder, and cook for about 2 minutes. Add potatoes, carrots, hominy, tomatoes, and chilis. Pour in beef broth. Season to taste with salt and pepper. Reduce heat, and simmer 2 hours or until potatoes and carrots are tender. Check for seasonings, and serve.

SPIKE BUCK SURPRISE

1 (16-ounce) package elbow macaroni

1 tablespoon canola oil

1 pound ground venison

1 onion, chopped

1 green bell pepper, chopped

1 can tomato paste

1 can diced tomatoes

¾ cup water

1 teaspoon salt

1 teaspoon garlic powder

¼ teaspoon pepper

1 (16-ounce) package shredded cheddar cheese

Preheat oven to 350 degrees. Spray a glass 9- by 13-inch baking dish with cooking spray. Bring a large pot of lightly salted water to a boil. Add pasta, and cook for 8 to 10 minutes or until al dente; drain. Meanwhile, heat canola oil in a large skillet over medium-high heat until it begins to smoke. Add venison, and cook, stirring to break apart, until browned and cooked through. Drain off any excess oil, then stir in onion and green pepper. Cook for a few minutes until the onion softens, then stir in tomato paste, diced tomatoes, and water until combined. Season with salt, garlic powder, and pepper. Stir together drained macaroni and tomato sauce, and pour into prepared baking dish. Bake in oven for 45 minutes, then sprinkle evenly with shredded cheddar cheese, and continue baking until the cheese is bubbly and browned, about 15 minutes.

EASY DEER AND JALAPEÑO SUMMER SAUSAGE

1 cup cold water
3 tablespoons sugar-based curing mixture
2 teaspoons mustard seed
1 teaspoon garlic powder
1 teaspoon coarse ground black pepper

2 teaspoons liquid smoke flavoring
3 pounds lean ground venison
1 cup shredded cheddar cheese
2 jalapeño peppers, seeded and minced

Stir the water, curing mixture, mustard seed, garlic powder, black pepper, and liquid smoke in a large bowl until the curing mixture has dissolved. Mix in the ground venison, cheddar cheese, and jalapeño peppers; mix until evenly blended and somewhat sticky, about 3 minutes. Divide the mixture in half, and roll each half into a 2-inch-thick log. Wrap each log tightly with aluminum foil, and refrigerate for 24 hours. Preheat an oven to 300 degrees. Line a baking sheet with aluminum foil, then remove the foil from the sausage logs and place them onto the baking sheet. Bake in oven until the internal temperature reaches 170 degrees, 1½ to 2 hours. Cool the sausages on a rack until they have cooled to room temperature. Dab occasionally with a paper towel to absorb excess grease. Slice thinly to serve. This is a fun recipe for young hunters!

SOGGY BRITCHES DEER BURGER LOAF

2 pounds ground venison
1 (6-ounce) package dry stuffing mix
1 cup water
1 onion, finely chopped

½ cup barbecue sauce, divided
2 large eggs, lightly beaten
Salt to taste
Black pepper to taste

Preheat oven to 375 degrees. Mix venison, stuffing mix, water, onion, ¼ cup barbecue sauce, eggs, salt, and black pepper together in a large bowl until fully incorporated. Shape venison mixture into a loaf, and place in a 9- by 13-inch baking dish. Spread remaining ¼ cup barbecue sauce over the top of loaf. Bake in oven until no longer pink in the center, about 1 hour. An instant-read thermometer inserted into the center should read at least 160 degrees. Goes great with fried taters!

DEER CHILI #1984

4 tablespoons bacon fat

1 large red onion, chopped fine

2 pounds coarsely ground venison

1 pound coarsely ground beef

3 pounds coarsely ground pork

3 tablespoons chili powder

1½ tablespoons cayenne pepper

1 tablespoon minced garlic

1½ teaspoons ground cumin

3 cans tomato sauce

2 cups water

1 can tomato paste

2 tablespoons paprika

2 tablespoons dried parsley

1 tablespoon garlic salt

½ teaspoon dried oregano

½ cup masa harina

Heat bacon fat in a 5-quart Dutch oven over medium heat. Add onion, and cook until tender, about 5 minutes. Add venison, and brown well, about 10 minutes. Brown beef in a separate skillet over medium heat, 7 to 10 minutes, then add it to Dutch oven with venison. Brown pork in skillet over medium heat, 10 to 15 minutes; add to Dutch oven with meat mixture, then add chili powder, cayenne pepper, garlic, and cumin. Cook over medium heat until flavors have combined, stirring occasionally, about 30 minutes. Stir tomato sauce, water, tomato paste, paprika, parsley, garlic salt, and oregano into the meat mixture in the Dutch oven. Bring to a boil. Reduce heat to a simmer, and cook for about 1 hour. Stir occasionally, and add water as needed. Mix masa harina into the meat mixture in the Dutch oven; cook until thickened, at least 30 minutes. Add more water as needed. I won Fin & Feather's chili competition with this recipe.

WINTER'S HUNT BREAKFAST SAUSAGE

6 pounds ground venison

2 pounds ground pork

¼ cup sugar-based curing mixture

1 tablespoon fresh-ground black pepper

1 tablespoon crushed red pepper flakes

¼ cup packed brown sugar

3 tablespoons dried sage

In a very large bowl or plastic tub, sprinkle the venison and pork with the curing mixture, pepper, pepper flakes, sugar, and sage. Mix well enough to evenly incorporate everything. When working with large quantities of sausage, cook a small piece to make sure the seasoning is exactly how you like it. Divide into 1-pound portions, and freeze. This makes great patties for a deer hunter's breakfast.

TASTY VENISON STROGANOFF

3 tablespoons olive oil
1 pound deer burger
1 teaspoon salt
1 teaspoon ground black pepper
1 teaspoon garlic powder

1 teaspoon onion powder
1 tablespoon all-purpose flour
1 cup water
1 can condensed cream of mushroom soup
1 (16 ounce) package uncooked egg noodles

Heat the olive oil in a large skillet over medium-high heat. Toss the ground venison with salt, pepper, garlic powder, and onion powder. Cook the venison in the hot oil until browned, about 8 minutes. Once browned, remove from the skillet, and place into a slow cooker, leaving remaining oil in the skillet. Reduce the heat on skillet to medium-low, and stir the flour into the remaining olive oil. Cook and stir until the flour has turned golden brown, about 5 minutes. Stir in the water, and bring to a simmer, then pour into the slow cooker along with the cream of mushroom soup. Cover, and cook on low for 1 hour. Bring a large pot of lightly salted water to a boil. Add the egg noodles, and cook al dente, 8 to 10 minutes. Drain, and then spoon the stroganoff over the egg noodles to serve. I have also made this recipe using stew meat, and it tastes great! Enjoy.

JEFF AND LINDA MAY'S OPENING DAY SAUSAGE PATTY RECIPE

1 pound ground venison

½ pound pepper bacon, cut into small pieces

1 teaspoon Accent Meat Tenderizer

1 tablespoon garlic powder

1 tablespoon onion powder

1 teaspoon ground mustard

1 tablespoon ground chipotle

1 teaspoon salt

1 teaspoon anise seed

1 teaspoon fennel seed

1 teaspoon crushed red pepper flakes

1 teaspoon dried parsley

Thoroughly combine the venison, bacon, Accent Meat Tenderizer, garlic powder, onion powder, ground mustard, chipotle, salt, anise, fennel, red pepper flakes, and parsley in a large bowl. Grind the mixture through a small plate in a meat grinder. Refrigerate until ready to use. This makes for great tasting breakfast patties on Opening Day.

COUSIN RICK'S DEER BURGER SOUP

1½ cups butter, divided

2 pounds deer burger

3 cups chopped cabbage

3 large potatoes, cubed

2 cans peas, drained

2 cans carrots, drained

2 cans green beans, drained

2 cans whole kernel corn, drained

2 cans diced tomatoes with juice

1 (64-ounce) bottle tomato juice

1 (32-ounce) container beef broth

2 tablespoons sugar

2 tablespoons beef bouillon granules

1 teaspoon salt

2 teaspoons ground black pepper

Pinch of ground cumin

Pinch of ground mustard

Pinch of curry powder

Pinch of cayenne pepper

Pinch of dried parsley

Pinch of Italian seasoning

Pinch of garlic powder

Melt ½ cup of butter in a large pot over medium-high heat. Brown the deer burger in the hot butter, stirring frequently. Add the cabbage, potatoes, peas, carrots, green beans, corn, diced tomatoes, and remaining 1 cup of butter. Pour in the tomato juice and beef broth, then sprinkle in the sugar, beef bouillon granules, salt, black pepper, cumin, mustard, curry powder, cayenne pepper, parsley, Italian seasoning, and garlic powder. Bring to a boil over high heat, then reduce heat to medium-low, cover, and simmer until the soup is slightly thickened, about 1½ hours.

DEER RUN DEER BURGER PIE

1 pound deer burger	1 can whole-kernel corn
1 small onion, chopped	1 (9-inch) pie crust
1 egg	2 cups prepared mashed potatoes
1 tablespoon ketchup	½ cup shredded cheddar cheese
1 tablespoon Worcestershire sauce	

Preheat oven to 350 degrees. In a skillet over medium heat, cook and stir the deer burger and onion until meat is evenly browned. Drain, and allow to cool slightly. In a bowl, mix the cooked deer burger and onion with egg, ketchup, and Worcestershire sauce. Spread the corn in the bottom of the pie crust. Layer with the deer burger mixture. Spoon the mashed potatoes over the deer meat, and top with cheese. Bake 30 minutes in oven until cheese is bubbly and lightly browned.

MRS. BECKY'S DEER BURGER MEATLOAF

5 carrots, peeled and sliced into 1-inch pieces	2 tablespoons tomato paste
1 large potato, peeled and cubed	2 pounds deer burger
1 large white onion, sliced into wedges	1 teaspoon dried thyme
3 stalks celery, cut into 2-inch pieces	1 teaspoon dried basil
1 large green bell pepper, seeded and cut into strips	1 teaspoon dried rosemary
4 cloves garlic, peeled	2 teaspoons cayenne pepper
4 eggs	1 teaspoon salt
3 tablespoons Dijon-style prepared mustard	1 teaspoon ground black pepper

Preheat oven to 375 degrees. Place carrots, potato, onion, celery, bell pepper, and garlic into a food processor, and purée to a wet paste. Add eggs, mustard, and tomato paste, and process for another few seconds. Place the deer burger in a large mixing bowl, and add puréed vegetable mixture, along with thyme, basil, rosemary, cayenne pepper, and salt and pepper. Knead together until thoroughly mixed. Form into two loaves, and place in a large baking dish. Bake for 50 to 60 minutes.

DEER BURGER RECIPE #1980

2 teaspoons canning salt

1 teaspoon chili powder

1 teaspoon garlic powder

1 teaspoon onion powder

¼ teaspoon ground ginger

¼ teaspoon ground black pepper

Pinch of cayenne pepper (optional)

1 pound deer burger

Stir salt, chili powder, garlic powder, onion powder, ginger, black pepper, and cayenne pepper together in a large bowl; add deer burger, and mix well. Pass deer burger mixture through a meat grinder set with the finest blade. Preheat oven to 250 degrees. Place wire racks onto baking sheets. Place half of the deer burger mixture between two sheets of heavy plastic on a solid, level surface. Firmly roll deer burger mixture to a thickness of ⅛ inch. Remove the top layer of plastic wrap, flip over the deer burger mixture onto prepared baking sheet, and remove the bottom layer of plastic wrap. Repeat for remaining deer burger mixture. Bake the deer burger mixture in oven with the oven door slightly ajar for 2½ hours. Rotate the baking sheet. Bake until jerky is cooked through, another 3 hours. Remove jerky from oven, and cut into strips while warm.

BUCK BURGER JERKY

½ cup soy sauce

1 teaspoon liquid smoke flavoring

½ teaspoon onion powder

½ teaspoon garlic powder (or 1 teaspoon minced garlic)

1 teaspoon sea salt

1 pound deer burger

In a glass bowl, combine all ingredients, and let sit in refrigerator for at least 4 hours. Load the mixture into a jerky-forming gun (if you have one), and use the gun to load your dehydrator trays. This mixture is fairly soft because of the added liquid, which makes it easier to fire through the gun. If you don't have a jerky gun, roll the mixture out very thinly (⅛-inch thick), and score lines where you would like the pieces to break apart. Dry at 145 to 165 degrees for 4 to 12 hours, until jerky is hard but still flexible and contains no pockets of moisture. For extra safety, heat finished jerky in a 275-degree oven for 10 minutes.

12-POINTER BALLS

MEATBALLS:

1 pound deer burger	1 teaspoon salt
½ cup uncooked white rice	½ teaspoon celery salt
½ cup water	⅛ teaspoon garlic powder
⅓ cup chopped onion	⅛ teaspoon ground black pepper

SAUCE:

1 (15-ounce) can tomato sauce	2 teaspoons Worcestershire sauce
1 cup water (or more as needed)	

Mix the deer burger, rice, ½ cup water, onion, salt, celery salt, garlic powder, and black pepper in a bowl. Roll the mixture into 12 meatballs. Heat a large skillet over medium-high heat, and add the meatballs. Cook meatballs, turning occasionally, until evenly browned. Drain, and discard any excess grease. For the sauce, pour the tomato sauce, 1 cup water, and Worcestershire sauce into the skillet; reduce heat to medium-low. Cover, and simmer until the meatballs are no longer pink in the center and the rice is tender, about 45 minutes. Stir in more water if the sauce becomes too dry.

SLOPPY DOES

2 pounds deer burger	2 tablespoons brown sugar
½ onion, diced	1 teaspoon Dijon mustard
2 cloves garlic, minced	1 dash Worcestershire sauce
1 green bell pepper, diced	1½ teaspoons salt (or to taste)
2 cups water, divided	½ teaspoon ground black pepper (or to taste)
¾ cup ketchup	1 pinch cayenne pepper, or to taste

Combine the deer burger and onion in a cold skillet, place the skillet onto a stove burner, and turn the heat to medium; cook and stir until the deer meat is crumbly and browned. Stir the garlic and bell pepper into the deer meat mixture; continue cooking and stirring until the vegetables are tender, 2 to 3 more minutes. Add 1 cup of water. Mix in ketchup, brown sugar, mustard, Worcestershire sauce, salt, and pepper. Pour in remaining 1 cup of water. Bring to a simmer. Reduce heat to low, and cook until the mixture becomes very thick, 30 to 45 minutes. Adjust salt and pepper as needed. Season with cayenne just before serving.

LONESOME TRAIL COWBOY BEANS

1 pound deer burger
½ pound bacon, minced
1 (28-ounce) can baked beans with pork
1 (15-ounce) can kidney beans, rinsed and drained
1 (15-ounce) can lima beans, rinsed and drained

2 onions, chopped
1 cup ketchup
1 cup brown sugar
1 teaspoon mustard

Heat a large cast iron skillet or Dutch oven over medium-high heat. Cook and stir the deer burger and bacon together in the hot skillet until deer burger is browned and crumbly, 7 to 10 minutes. In the crock of your slow cooker, add deer burger and bacon, then stir in baked beans with pork, kidney beans, lima beans, onions, ketchup, brown sugar, and mustard until everything is well mixed. Cook on low until hot and thickened, at least 3 hours.

CHAPTER 6

Wild Bird Cooking: Wild Turkey, Pheasant, Duck, Goose, Quail, and Grouse

If you're like me, you really get bummed out the moment back home after a bird hunt when you carry in your bag of pheasants and waterfowl knowing that the next step is cleaning. But after all these years, I've since discovered a good method for plucking fowl. You see, once the bird is cold, the roots of the feathers become locked in the tightened flesh, so when the critter is plucked, bits of skin come off. To reduce tearing of the skin, just use wet heat, like a quick scalding.

To remove the feathers, you'll first need a pot or kettle that's big enough to allow you to submerge the bird entirely. Fill the vat at least to the halfway point with water, and set it on the stove. (If you have only one or two birds to pluck, you can probably work in the camp kitchen. When there's a whole mess of feathered fowl to be processed, though, you might want to build an outdoor fire to make cleanup easier.) While the water is heating, add two tablespoons of dishwashing detergent for each bucketful of liquid—the cleaner decreases the surface tension of the water and allows it to penetrate the feathers more thoroughly.

Now, let the water reach a temperature of about 160 degrees. (Any hotter than scalding could cause the bird's skin to tear, but too little heat will make the feathers difficult to pull free.) Then dunk the carcass head first (hold the feet) into the hot bath for 90 seconds. If your pot is large enough, draw the bird backwards through the water while it's submerged in order to force the heated liquid through the feathers and under the wings for a more thorough soaking. Then let the birds drain on sheets of clean paper towels or newspaper.

At this point, most hunters will begin the task of tugging out the feathers. However, I've found that even after dipping the bird in hot water, the skin may still tear, so be very careful. Another great tip is to simply soak a few medium towels in the hot water and tuck one of the compresses under each wing. Then, with the towels still in place, place the whole drenched bird into a plastic bag to help retain the heat and moisture.

Keep the bird in the bag for about 25 minutes before carefully unwrapping. While the fowl is still warm, you can begin plucking the wing feathers. Always remove the feathers by pulling steadily on the quills rather than jerking them out, and be sure to pluck in the direction in which the feathers lie.

After the bird, has been plucked over once, you'll need to pull off any remaining pinfeathers. For removing them, try a long pair of tweezers.

Cooking with Wild Turkey

SPRING GOBBLER CHILI

3 tablespoons vegetable oil, divided
2 pounds wild turkey meat, cubed
1 (1-ounce) package taco seasoning mix
1 teaspoon ground coriander
1 teaspoon dried oregano
1 teaspoon chili pepper flakes
2 tablespoons tomato paste
1 can beef broth
1 cup salsa

1 can crushed tomatoes, or coarsely chopped tomatoes packed in purée
1 (7-ounce) can chopped green chili peppers
1 white onion, finely chopped
1 green bell pepper, diced
2 zucchini, halved lengthwise and sliced
1 cup chopped green onions
Sour cream
Shredded cheddar cheese

Heat 1 tablespoon of oil in a large stockpot over medium-high heat. Add the wild turkey meat into the pot, stirring with a wooden spoon to brown all sides. Season with taco seasoning mix, coriander, oregano, chili flakes, and tomato paste, and mix until meat is evenly coated with seasonings. Continue cooking, reducing heat if necessary, until turkey is well browned. Pour in beef broth, and simmer to reduce liquid slightly, about 5 minutes. Add salsa, tomatoes, and green chilis, and continue cooking at a moderate simmer for 10 minutes. Adjust the thickness at any time by adding water. While chili is still cooking, heat 1 tablespoon of oil in a large skillet over medium-high heat. Cook onion and green bell pepper, stirring occasionally, for 5 minutes, or until onion is translucent and bell pepper is lightly browned. Add onion and bell pepper to the chili, and continue cooking at a very low simmer. In the same skillet, heat the remaining tablespoon of oil over medium-high heat. Add the zucchini, and cook, stirring occasionally, for 5 minutes or until lightly browned. Add the zucchini to the chili, reduce heat, and continue cooking 15 minutes more. Again, adjust the consistency with water as needed. Check for seasonings, and ladle chili into serving bowls. Top with green onions, sour cream, and cheddar cheese, and then serve.

GOBBLER CAMP SOUP

½ cup butter

1 cup all-purpose flour

11 cups water

3 cubes chicken bouillon

2 pounds wild turkey meat cut into bite-size pieces

2 heads fresh broccoli, cut into florets

1½ teaspoons salt

1 teaspoon ground black pepper

1 cup light cream

3 cups shredded cheddar cheese

In a 5-quart pot, melt butter over medium heat. Mix in flour, stirring constantly until a thick paste forms. Remove from pot, and set aside. In the same pot, combine water, bouillon cubes, wild turkey chunks, broccoli, salt, and pepper. Bring to a boil over high heat. Reduce heat to medium-low, and simmer for 45 minutes. Stir in the flour mixture a little bit at a time until soup thickens. Simmer 5 minutes. Reduce heat, and stir in cream. Mix in cheese 1 cup at a time, and stir until melted. Check for seasonings, and serve hot. This is a very good wild turkey soup. Try it!

MOSER'S CABIN WILD TURKEY BREAST

1 wild turkey breast

2 tablespoons butter, softened

¼ cup whipped cream cheese spread

with garden vegetables

1 tablespoon soy sauce

1 tablespoon minced fresh parsley

½ teaspoon dried basil

½ teaspoon dried sage

½ teaspoon dried thyme

¼ teaspoon ground black pepper

¼ teaspoon garlic powder

Place the wild turkey breast into a slow cooker. Combine butter, whipped cream cheese spread, soy sauce, parsley, basil, sage, thyme, black pepper, and garlic powder in a small bowl until smooth. Brush herb mixture over the turkey breast. Cover slow cooker. Cook until tender, 4 to 6 hours on high or 8 to 10 hours on low.

TUMA LAKE HUNTING LODGE WILD TURKEY & DEER STEW

4 pounds wild turkey breast, cut into 1-inch pieces

2 pounds red potatoes, cut in 1-inch pieces

1 pound deer stew meat, cut into bite-size pieces

1 (16-ounce) package frozen whole kernel corn

1 package frozen cut carrots

1 can cut green beans, drained

1 can chicken broth

8 ounces diced celery

1 can beef broth

1 (14.5-ounce) can petite diced tomatoes

8 ounces diced onion

8 ounces diced green bell pepper

8 ounces shredded cabbage

¼ cup salt (or to taste)

2 tablespoons dried basil

2 tablespoons dried oregano

2 tablespoons celery salt

1 tablespoon ground black pepper

1 packet concentrated vegetable base

Mix all ingredients in a slow cooker. Cook on low for 6 hours. Check several times for taste before serving this great tasting hunter's stew.

GRANDPA BLACK'S FAVORITE GRILLED GOBBLER

2 cloves garlic, peeled and minced

1 tablespoon finely chopped fresh basil

½ teaspoon ground black pepper

2 wild turkey breast halves

6 whole cloves

¼ cup vegetable oil

¼ cup soy sauce

2 tablespoons lemon juice

1 tablespoon brown sugar

In a small bowl, mix together the garlic, basil, and pepper. Rub over the wild turkey breasts. Insert one clove into each end of the turkey breasts, and one in the center. In a large shallow dish, blend vegetable oil, soy sauce, lemon juice, and brown sugar. Place the breasts in the dish, and turn to coat. Cover, and marinate in the refrigerator at least 4 hours. Preheat grill for high heat. Lightly oil the grill grate. Discard marinade, and place turkey breasts on the grill. Close the lid, and grill turkey breasts about 15 minutes on each side, to an internal temperature of 170 degrees. For me, this recipe always brings back fond memories of grandpa standing in front of his old grill talking about the hunt.

LEWIS & CLARK DUTCH OVEN TOM

1 whole bone-in Tom turkey breast with skin

1½ cups chicken stock

6 tablespoons butter, melted

2 teaspoons chicken bouillon granules

1 teaspoon dried sage

1 teaspoon dried savory

1 teaspoon dried rosemary

1 teaspoon dried thyme

Preheat oven to 350 degrees. Loosen the skin from the meat of the wild turkey breast. Place the turkey breast into a Dutch oven with a lid, and pour chicken stock over the meat. Mix melted butter with chicken bouillon granules, sage, savory, rosemary, and thyme in a bowl. Lift the loosened skin, and pour slightly more than half the butter-herb mixture under the skin. Pour remaining herb mixture over the skin. Cover the Dutch oven. Roast in the oven for about 3 hours; flip the wild turkey breast over, and roast 1 more hour; flip again, and roast until the juices run clear, 1 additional hour (5 hours in all). An instant-read meat thermometer inserted into the thickest part of the breast (not touching bone) should read 180 degrees. Baste the Tom with pan drippings, and let stand 15 minutes before serving.

GOBBLERS IN THE GARLIC DUTCH OVEN WILD TURKEY

2 tablespoons butter

1 tablespoon olive oil

1 large wild turkey breast

10 cloves garlic

¼ cup water

2 tablespoons lemon juice

1 teaspoon salt

½ teaspoon dried thyme

¼ teaspoon ground black pepper

Preheat oven to 350 degrees. Melt the butter with the olive oil in a large Dutch oven over medium-high heat. Add the turkey breast to the Dutch oven, and brown on all sides in the butter and oil, 5 to 10 minutes. Remove the turkey to a cutting board. Drain all but 2 tablespoons of liquid from the pan; stir the garlic cloves into the reserved liquid. Return the wild turkey to the pan; sprinkle the water, lemon juice, salt, thyme, and black pepper over the bird, and cover tightly. Bake the gobbler in oven until no longer pink at the bone and the juices run clear, about 90 minutes. An instant-read thermometer inserted into the thickest part of the meat should read 180 degrees. Remove the gobbler from the oven, cover with a doubled sheet of aluminum foil, and allow to rest in a warm area for 15 minutes before slicing.

SMOKED WILD TURKEY

1 good-size wild turkey
1 cup rub of your choice (see rubs on pages 6 to 8)
1 cup sugar

1 tablespoon garlic, minced
½ cup Worcestershire sauce
2 tablespoons canola oil

Thaw turkey if you froze it after the hunt. On the day before cooking, pour 3 gallons of water in a 5-gallon non-metal bucket. Add your favorite barbecue rub, and mix until completely dissolved. Next add sugar, garlic, and Worcestershire sauce. Submerge wild turkey in bucket. Refrigerate turkey in bucket overnight.

Place grill on high smoke, and smoke turkey for 3 hours. Switch grilling temp to 350 degrees. Push a metal meat thermometer into the thickest part of the breast, about ¾ inch away from the bone. Push it straight down into the bird until it touches the bone, and then back it out about ½ inch. Leave the thermometer in. Cook another 4 hours or so until the internal temperature of the turkey is 165 degrees. Take off grill. Let rest 15 to 20 minutes before slicing.

CHEF SAGE ISLAND-STYLE TURKEY JERK

1 teaspoon finely chopped onion
3 tablespoons brown sugar
4 tablespoons soy sauce
4 tablespoons red wine vinegar
2 teaspoons chopped fresh thyme
1 teaspoon sesame oil

3 cloves garlic, chopped
½ teaspoon ground allspice
1 habanero pepper, sliced
1 boneless wild turkey breast,
halved and cut into 1-inch strips

Combine the onion, brown sugar, soy sauce, vinegar, thyme, sesame oil, garlic, allspice, and habanero pepper in the container of a food processor or blender. Process until smooth. Place the wild turkey meat into a large resealable bag, and pour in three-quarters of the sauce. Squeeze out excess air, and seal. Marinate in the refrigerator for at least 1 hour. Preheat your oven's broiler. Remove turkey from bag, and discard marinade. Broil the turkey meat for 10 to 15 minutes, turning once to ensure even cooking. Heat remaining sauce in a small pan, and pour over turkey meat when serving. I want to thank Chef Sage from Montego Bay, Jamaica, for helping me develop these great flavors from an American wild game bird. We knocked it out of the park on this recipe and had fun doing it!

COUSIN RICK'S TURKEY BOW-HUNTING TIPS

If you're like me, you love turkey hunting with a bow. I find the thrill is undeniably better than bow-hunting big game like deer. And you'll love it even more if you follow these great tips on wild turkey hunting. Pass them along to your buddies, and use them to instruct young bow hunters. Remember, as with most hunting, the work begins in the off-season. I want to personally thank Vinny Moser and Jeff May for most of these great tips. Those old boys are well-seasoned gobbler bow hunters!

1. Scout. Bow-hunting turkeys is similar to bow-hunting deer. You do not have the luxury of using run-and-gun tactics like the shotgun hunter does. You must know the land, how the gobblers are using the land, and how to ambush the turkeys from natural cover or a ground blind. Learn where the birds will be, then figure out how you can set up in the area without being detected. You may be surprised how easy it is to kill a bird with a bow on the first or second sit of the year when you're armed with this information.

2. Use a Decoy. Once you have pinpointed a place to set up your blind or a place that offers natural cover to shoot from, think about buying a decoy or two. A decoy attracts the birds to your location and will take their eyes off you. Place the decoys close (5 to 10 yards away) and out of the line of sight of your location. From your scouting, you should know where the birds are likely to approach from.

3. Learn to Use a Mouth Call. Like my old buddy Vince Moser taught me, you can't shoot a bow holding a call, so the hands-free diaphragm calls are a necessity. Pick one up and learn to make the basic yelp, purr, and cut. But calling is not a substitute for scouting. No matter how good a turkey caller you are, you can't call a bird where he does not want to go. Use calls to get the attention of turkeys and trigger them to search for or pursue your decoys.

4. Tune Your Bow and Choose Your Broadhead with Turkeys in Mind. I learned the hard way that turkeys are a much different target than big game animals, so you should adjust accordingly. Think close shots and large cutting diameter broadheads to make sure you'll hit their small vitals. You want to get the turkeys close, and combining decoys with good woodsmanship and calling will present a shot closer than you ever thought possible.

5. Practice Your Turkey Shots Under Hunting Conditions. Get a life-sized turkey target, and make sure you know the best shot placement for turkeys. Practice from a hunting stool, and in standing, kneeling, and sitting positions until you are sure your form is solid and you can consistently hit the target with the broadhead on every release.

With a little preparation and the right archery, decoy, and calling gear, getting a close shot on a turkey can be easier than you think. Don't be intimidated by talk about how hard bow-hunting supposedly is. Just put down the gun, stay focused on where the birds will be, and make your shot count. Then you can kick back and enjoy your harvest with all these great tasting recipes I have for you! Be safe, and be smart!

Cooking with Pheasant

PAN-FRIED PHEASANT

3 pheasants, split
½ cup butter
2 cups sliced button mushrooms
1 cup dry white wine

2 tablespoons lemon juice
½ cup chopped onion
1 teaspoon salt
1 teaspoon pepper

Sauté pheasants in butter for 10 minutes. Remove from skillet, and sauté mushrooms in remaining butter in skillet for 10 minutes. Return pheasant to skillet, then add wine, lemon juice, onions, salt, and pepper. Cover, and simmer 1 hour or until tender.

KING'S AND QUEEN'S BREAST OF PHEASANT

6 pheasant breasts
6 slices bacon
2 cloves garlic, roughly chopped
½ teaspoon grated ginger root

1 (10-ounce) bottle Russian salad dressing
Salt to taste
Ground black pepper to taste
2 green onions, chopped

Heat a large cast iron skillet over medium-high heat. Sauté pheasant breasts until well browned on both sides. Allow pheasant to cool slightly. Wrap each breast in a piece of bacon, and place in a slow cooker. Sprinkle garlic and ginger over the pheasant; top with Russian dressing. Cook on low heat for 5 to 6 hours. Season to taste with salt and pepper, and garnish with green onions.

MOSSBERG PHEASANT BREASTS

4 tablespoons butter, divided

1 onion, chopped

8 fresh mushrooms, thinly sliced

1 clove garlic, chopped

¼ pound thinly sliced prosciutto, cut into strips

¼ pound thinly sliced hard salami, cut into strips

4 pheasant breast halves

1 cup all-purpose flour

Salt to taste

Ground black pepper to taste

½ cup dry sherry

1 cup chicken broth

½ cup heavy cream

½ cup marinara sauce

2 tablespoons chopped fresh parsley

Melt 3 tablespoons butter in a large cast iron skillet over medium heat. Sauté onion until soft and translucent. Stir in mushrooms, garlic, prosciutto, and salami. Dredge the pheasant breasts in flour, and place in pan. Season with salt and pepper. Cook pheasant 5 minutes on each side. Pour in sherry, and cook until liquid is reduced by half. Stir in chicken broth, cream, and marinara. Simmer until sauce is reduced to your preferred consistency. Stir in remaining 1 tablespoon butter, and sprinkle with parsley. Check again for seasonings, and serve. A great meal for your hungry bird-hunting buddies!

BUBBA GOT SMOKED PHEASANT

1 whole pheasant

1 tablespoon garlic powder

4 cups lemon-lime flavored soda (such as 7-Up)

2 cups wood chips, soaked

Place the pheasant into a large zippered plastic bag. Sprinkle in garlic powder, then pour in enough lemon-lime soda to cover the bird. Seal the bag, and place in the refrigerator overnight to marinate. Light charcoal in an outdoor smoker, and wait until the temperature is at 225 degrees. Remove the pheasant from the bag, and place on the grill grate. Discard marinade. Cover, and cook for 10 hours. Occasionally toss a handful of soaked wood chips on the coals. Check for seasonings, and serve. This is a fun, easy recipe that is great for teaching kids the art of wild game cooking.

COUSIN RICK'S PHEASANT HUNTING TIPS

Pheasant hunting is a great way to teach young hunters field safety—plus it's a blast to do! These six pheasant-hunting tips for beginners will get you started on the right foot.

Be Very, Very Quiet. As a big-time deer hunter, I am meticulous about closing doors quietly. The slam of a truck door will alert pheasants in the same way it would a whitetail. Pheasants have pretty good hearing, and when they feel threatened, they'll hunker down or head for thicker cover. You can get away with talking softly, but close doors quietly and use hand signals as much as possible.

Don't Rush. I have learned the hard way that a lot of old roosters earn their years thanks to the impatience of hunters. Hunters often move through cover too fast, allowing pheasants to circle behind them and into safety.

Work through cover in a zigzag fashion, and try pausing frequently, which is a good way to get roosters to flush. Sometimes, a brief stop is just enough to get a bird holding tight to lose confidence and take to the skies.

Hunt the Edges. Pheasants move through various types of habitat throughout the day. This movement leaves them holding to edges frequently. A lot of hunters target big chunks of habitat, but it is important to check out places like fence lines and ditches. Anywhere one type of pheasant habitat transitions to another can offer excellent hunting.

Hit Snooze and Get Some Sleep. The early bird gets the worm, right? Well, the early bird gets hungry later in the day too. Many pheasant hunters have their feet by the fire by late afternoon, but they could be missing the best hunting of the day. Pheasants start moving out of heavy cover and into more open roost sites during the last hour of daylight. Grassy patches along cornfields are classic cover spots for evening ringnecks.

Try Late-Season Hunting. The same hunters that are sitting fireside for happy hour usually put their shotguns away before the snow flies too. But late-season pheasant hunting can be very good, and hunters willing to brave the elements are often rewarded with heavy game vests. Cattail marshes are my favorite cover for late-season pheasant hunting. They don't get any pressure early in the year, but once the water has frozen into ice that is thick enough to walk on, you can move through cattails easier, and the birds gravitate to them.

Bring a Friend. One of the great things about pheasant hunting is the social aspect. Hunting pheasants is tough to do by yourself, so most experienced hunters are more than happy to have someone join in on the fun, even if they are new to the game. State wildlife agencies often bolster wild pheasant populations with farm-raised birds, but if you're looking for a higher-quality experience, book a hunt with a guide or at a pheasant-hunting ranch. This will get you out of the house—and maybe the state—for a great time in the field. Have a great hunt, and enjoy the great tasting recipes I have for you in this chapter.

ZANGGER'S COUNTRY FANCY PHEASANT

½ pound baby red potatoes, cut in half

1 zucchini, halved lengthwise and cut into 1-inch slices

1 red onion, cut into ½-inch-thick wedges

2 red bell peppers, cut into 1-inch pieces

12 cherry tomatoes

2 tablespoons minced garlic

½ teaspoon dried thyme leaves

¼ teaspoon crushed red pepper flakes

Salt to taste

Freshly ground black pepper to taste

2 tablespoons olive oil

4 pheasant breast halves

4 slices thinly sliced prosciutto di Parma

Preheat oven to 400 degrees. Mix potatoes, zucchini, onion, bell peppers, and tomatoes into a large bowl; add garlic, thyme, and red pepper flakes. Toss vegetable mixture, and season with salt and pepper. Pour olive oil over the vegetables, and toss to coat; pour into a glass baking dish. Roast vegetables in oven until tender, about 15 minutes. Season pheasant breasts with salt and pepper. Wrap each breast with a slice of prosciutto, and secure prosciutto in place with toothpicks; place atop the vegetables, and continue baking until the pheasant has firmed and is no longer pink in the center, about 30 minutes. Remove pheasant from the baking dish to cool for 5 minutes. Divide the roasted vegetables between 2 dinner plates. Remove toothpicks from pheasant; cut each piece into 5 diagonal slices. Fan the pheasant out on top of the vegetables. Check again for seasonings, and then serve.

MIKE AND SALLY'S IOWA PHEASANT SOUP AND NOODLES

1 cup chopped celery

¼ cup chopped onion

¼ cup butter (or margarine)

4 cups chopped, cooked pheasant breast meat

¼ cup chopped carrots

12 cups water

9 cubes chicken bouillon

½ teaspoon dried marjoram

½ teaspoon ground black pepper

1 bay leaf

1 tablespoon dried parsley

8 ounces egg noodles

In a large stockpot, sauté celery and onion in butter or margarine. Add pheasant, carrots, water, bouillon cubes, marjoram, black pepper, bay leaf, and parsley. Simmer for 30 minutes. Add noodles, and simmer for 10 more minutes. Check for seasonings, and serve.

PHEASANT "OLD WORLD" SCHNITZEL

1 tablespoon olive oil (plus more for drizzling)
6 pheasant breasts, cut in half lengthwise (butterflied)
Salt and to taste
Ground black pepper to taste
¾ cup all-purpose flour

1 tablespoon paprika
2 eggs, beaten
2 cups seasoned bread crumbs
1 large lemon, zested

Preheat oven to 425 degrees. Line a large baking sheet with aluminum foil, and drizzle olive oil over foil. Place baking sheet in oven. Flatten pheasant breasts so they are all about ¼-inch thick. Season pheasant with salt and pepper. Mix flour and paprika together on a large plate. Beat eggs with salt and pepper in a shallow bowl. Mix bread crumbs and lemon zest together on a separate large plate. Dredge each pheasant piece in flour mixture, then in egg, and then in bread crumbs, and set aside in 1 layer on a clean plate. Remove baking sheet from oven, and arrange pheasant breasts in a single layer on the sheet. Drizzle more olive oil over each piece of coated bird. Bake in oven for 5 to 6 minutes. Flip pheasant, and continue baking until no longer pink in the center and the breading is lightly browned, 5 to 6 minutes more. An instant-read thermometer inserted into the center should read at least 165 degrees.

"That's one powerful duck call ya got there, Cousin."

Cooking with Duck

LARSON'S WILD DUCK

2 teaspoons salt

1 teaspoon freshly ground black pepper

1 tablespoon dried thyme leaves

1 tablespoon crushed dried rosemary

5 potatoes, cubed

4 tablespoons olive oil

4 cups frozen blueberries

½ cup water

½ cup apple juice

½ cup sugar

1 jalapeño pepper, finely chopped

3 slices pancetta or bacon, cut into thin strips

6 shallots, thinly sliced

½ cup sliced shiitake mushrooms

2 pounds bok choy, sliced

4 wild duck breast halves

2 tablespoons vegetable oil

1 tablespoon butter

2 tablespoons aged balsamic vinegar

Preheat oven to 375 degrees. In a bowl, mix together the salt, black pepper, thyme, and rosemary; set aside. This will be your spice blend for seasoning the roasted potatoes and the wild duck breasts. Place cubed potatoes into a baking dish. Drizzle with olive oil, and sprinkle 2 tablespoons of your spice blend over the top of the potatoes. Toss potatoes in the pan until evenly coated with oil and seasonings. Spread into a single layer across the bottom of the baking dish, and bake for about 45 minutes in oven. While the potatoes are roasting, stir together the blueberries, water, apple juice, sugar, and jalapeño in a small saucepan. Bring to a boil over medium-high heat, then reduce heat to low, and simmer until mixture has reduced to the consistency of syrup, about 10 minutes. Cook the pancetta in a large skillet over medium heat until crispy. Remove pancetta to drain on a paper towel, leaving the drippings in the skillet. Add the shallots and mushrooms to the hot skillet; stir and cook until soft and just beginning to brown. Remove shallots and mushrooms, and set aside. Increase heat to medium-high, and place the bok choy in the hot skillet. Stir and cook bok choy until the leaves are wilted and white stalk pieces are tender, about 5 minutes. Return shallots, mushrooms, and pancetta to the skillet, turn off heat, and set aside. Rinse the duck breast halves, and pat dry. Rub remaining spice blend onto both sides of the duck breasts. Preheat a large skillet over medium-high heat, and when the pan is hot, put in the vegetable oil and butter. Immediately place the duck breasts in the pan, skin and fat side down. Do not move the duck breasts until the skin is deep brown, about 5 minutes. Turn the breasts, and cook until the internal temperature of the thickest part is 165 degrees. Remove duck from the pan, and place on a plate, covered with foil, to rest for 5 minutes. While the duck is resting, place the skillet with the bok choy mixture onto a burner over medium heat to warm through. Slice each duck breast diagonally into ½-inch strips. Divide the bok choy mixture among four plates, and drizzle each serving with ½ tablespoon of aged balsamic vinegar. Arrange sliced duck breasts on top of the bok choy mixture; ladle on blueberry sauce. As always, check for seasonings. Serve with oven-roasted potatoes on the side.

MISSISSIPPI RIVER BLIND ROASTED DUCK

2 teaspoons salt
1 teaspoon black pepper
2 teaspoons paprika

1 large wild duck (I prefer mallards)
½ cup butter, melted and divided

Preheat oven to 375 degrees. Rub salt, pepper, and paprika into the skin of the wild duck. Place in a roasting pan. Roast duck in oven for 1 hour. Spoon ¼ cup melted butter over the duck, and continue cooking for 45 more minutes. Spoon remaining ¼ cup melted butter over duck, and cook for 20 more minutes, or until golden brown. Check for seasonings, and serve with wild rice.

FARMLANDS LAKE ITALIAN DUCK

2 teaspoons olive oil, divided
4 Italian turkey sausage links, casings removed
1 medium onion, diced
3 cloves garlic, minced
½ cup pearl barley
1 cup green lentils

2 bone-in duck breast halves, skin removed
½ cup chopped fresh parsley
3 cups chicken stock
1 (15-ounce) can chickpeas, drained
1 (16-ounce) bag fresh spinach leaves, chopped
1 cup mild salsa

Heat 1 teaspoon olive oil in a pressure cooker over medium heat. Add sausage meat, and cook until browned, breaking it into crumbles. Transfer sausage to a paper towel–lined plate, and allow excess oil to drain. Add another 1 teaspoon of olive oil to pressure cooker; cook onion and garlic until onion is translucent. Add barley, and stir 1 minute. Return sausage to pressure cooker. Add lentils, duck, parsley, and chicken stock to cooker, adding enough stock to completely cover duck. Close cover securely; place pressure regulator on vent pipe. Bring pressure cooker to full pressure over high heat. Reduce heat to medium-high; cook for about 9 minutes. Pressure regulator should maintain a slow, steady rocking motion; adjust heat if necessary. Remove pressure cooker from heat; use quick-release following manufacturer's instructions, or allow pressure to drop on its own. Open cooker, and remove duck; shred meat, and return to soup. Add chickpeas, spinach, and salsa, stirring to blend and heating through before serving. Check again for seasonings, and enjoy your bird!

COUSIN RICK'S GRILLED DUCK

¼ cup Worcestershire sauce

2 tablespoons olive oil

½ teaspoon hot sauce

2 tablespoons minced garlic

¼ teaspoon black pepper

8 skinned, boned duck breast halves

Stir together the Worcestershire sauce, olive oil, hot sauce, garlic, and pepper. Add the duck breasts, and toss well to coat. Cover, and marinate in the refrigerator for at least 30 minutes to overnight. Preheat a grill for medium-high heat. Grill the duck to desired doneness, about 5 minutes per side for medium-well, depending on the size of the breast, and the temperature of the grill. Check for seasonings, and serve. Great with an ice-cold brew!

Cousin Rick's Deer Camp Quickies

Q: What's the difference between beer nuts and deer nuts?

A: Beer nuts are $1.25 but deer nuts are always under a buck.

Q: How do you save a deer during hunting season?

A: You hang on for deer life.

Q: What do you call a deer with no eyes?

A: I have no I-deer.

Q: What do you call a deer with no eyes and no legs?

A: Still no eye-deer.

Q: What do you call a deer with no eyes, no legs, and no balls?

A: Still no dang eye-deer.

Q: What did the doe say to the 24-point buck?

A: Boy you're horny!

PLANK ROAD DUCK VITTLES FOR HUNTERS

1½ cups plain yogurt

3 tablespoons lemon juice

2 tablespoons ground turmeric

2 tablespoons garam masala

2 tablespoons ground cumin

3 pounds bone-in duck with skin

1 cup water

1 cup basmati rice

¼ teaspoon kosher salt

½ cup unsalted butter

2 large onions, peeled and chopped

3 tablespoons grated fresh ginger root

4 cloves garlic, sliced

1 tablespoon cumin seeds

2 tablespoons tomato paste

2 fresh tomatoes, chopped

2 Anaheim chili peppers, seeded and diced

1 cinnamon stick

1 cup chicken stock

1 can coconut milk

1 bunch cilantro, finely chopped

Stir yogurt, lemon juice, turmeric, garam masala, and ground cumin together in a large bowl. Nestle the duck meat into the yogurt mixture, and turn to coat. Cover with plastic wrap, and marinate in the refrigerator, 4 hours to overnight. Combine water, rice, and salt in an electric pressure cooker. Close, and lock the lid. Select high pressure according to manufacturer's instructions; set timer for 6 minutes. Allow 10 to 15 minutes for pressure to build. Release pressure using the natural-release method, 10 to 40 minutes. Preheat oven to 250 degrees. Transfer rice to an oven-safe bowl; keep warm in the oven until ready to serve. Melt butter in the cooker on the sauté function. Add onions, ginger, garlic, and cumin seeds. Sauté, stirring frequently, until onions are softened and translucent, about 5 minutes. Stir in tomato paste for 1 minute. Add tomatoes, chili peppers, and cinnamon stick; cook and stir until chilis are softened, about 12 minutes. Place the duck meat, marinade, and chicken stock into the pot. Close, and lock the lid. Select high pressure according to manufacturer's instructions. Cook until duck is no longer pink at the bone and the juices run clear, about 20 minutes. Allow 10 to 15 minutes for pressure to build. Release pressure using the natural-release method according to manufacturer's instructions, 10 to 40 minutes. Transfer the duck meat to an oven-safe bowl; place in the oven to keep warm. Switch pressure cooker back to sauté function, and bring sauce to a boil. Cook until reduced by one-third, about 10 minutes. Stir in coconut milk, and cook until heated through, about 1 minute. Scoop rice into each bowl; add cooked duck meat. Ladle sauce over it all, and top with cilantro. This is a long recipe, so take your time—it'll be worth it. Great tasting vittles!

DUCK BLIND SOUP

2 large ducks (about 3 pounds)
½ cup white rice
Salt to taste

Freshly ground black pepper to taste
3 eggs, beaten
2 lemons, juiced

Rinse the ducks, and place in a pot large enough for the ducks to move around, but don't leave too much room or the broth will be watery. Fill with enough water to cover ducks by about 1 inch. Cover, and bring to a boil. When boiling, reduce heat to low, and simmer for 45 minutes to 1 hour, skimming the fat from the top as it collects. When the duck is done, the meat should pull from the bones easily. Transfer the duck meat to a large bowl, and set aside to cool. Add the rice to the pot, and season the broth with salt and pepper. Simmer over low heat for 20 more minutes or until rice is tender. Whisk the eggs with the lemon juice in a bowl. When the rice is done, turn off the heat. Whisk 1 ladle full of hot broth into the eggs slowly so the eggs do not curdle. Gradually whisk in more broth until the egg mixture is heated. Then pour the egg mixture back into the pot, whisking briskly. The result should be a creamy, cloudy-looking soup. Make sure to double check seasonings before serving.

"UNDER PRESSURE" COOKER DUCK AND SAUCE

DUCKS:

1 tablespoon olive oil

3 wild ducks, cut into pieces

Salt to taste

Ground black pepper to taste

½ teaspoon paprika

½ teaspoon dried marjoram

¼ cup white wine

¼ cup chicken broth

DUCK SAUCE:

¼ cup apricot preserves

2 tablespoons white vinegar

1½ teaspoons minced fresh ginger root

2 tablespoons honey

Heat the olive oil in the pressure cooker with the lid off, over medium-high heat. Add duck meat, and brown on all sides as evenly as possible. Remove duck from the cooker, and season with salt, pepper, paprika, and marjoram. Drain and discard fat from the cooker, and mix in wine and chicken broth, scraping any bits of food that are stuck to the bottom. Return duck meat to the cooker over medium-high heat, secure the lid, and bring to high pressure for 8 minutes or until the bird meat is tender. Reduce pressure before opening the lid. The internal temperature of the duck meat should be 180 degrees. Transfer duck to a serving dish, and add the apricot preserves, vinegar, ginger, and honey to the pot. Bring to a boil, and cook uncovered until the sauce has reduced into a thick and syrupy consistency, about 10 minutes. Spoon over duck, and serve. Mmm, mmm, good!

A duck, a skunk, and a deer went out for dinner at a restaurant one night. When it came time to pay, the skunk didn't have a scent, the deer didn't have a buck, so they put the meal on the duck's bill.

THE MOTHER OF ALL GAME BIRD FEASTS

1 whole pheasant, boned

Salt to taste

Ground black pepper to taste

Creole seasoning to taste

1 whole wild duck, boned

1 large wild turkey, boned

3 cups prepared sausage and oyster dressing

24 cans ice-cold beer

Preheat oven to 375 degrees. Lay the boned pheasant skin-side down on a platter, and season liberally with salt, pepper, and Creole seasoning. Lay the boned duck skin-side down on top of the pheasant, and again season liberally with salt, pepper, and Creole seasoning. Cover and refrigerate. Lay the boned turkey skin-side down on a flat surface. Cover it with a layer of cold sausage and oyster dressing, and push the dressing into the leg and wing cavities so they look as if they still have bones in them. Lay the duck on top of the turkey skin-side down, and cover it with a layer of cold dressing. Then, lay the pheasant on top of the duck skin-side down, and cover it too with a layer of cold dressing. With the help of a hunting buddy or junior chef, bring the edges of the turkey skin up, and fasten them together with toothpicks. Use kitchen string to lace around the toothpicks and hold the stuffed turkey together. Carefully place the beast breast up in a large roasting pan. Roast covered for 4 hours or until the monster bird is golden brown. Check the Godzilla every few hours to baste and remove excess liquid. There will be enough pan juices for tons of gravy. Continue to roast uncovered for 1 hour or until a meat thermometer inserted through the thigh registers 180 degrees and a thermometer inserted through the stuffing registers 165 degrees. Carve and serve. Oh, that beer in the ingredients isn't for the recipe—it's for you and your hunting buddies to drink while you create this mother of all game birds! This recipe is worth every cent you paid for this book, and it's sure to be a hit at the next hunt, wild game feed, or sporting event you cook at. People will write songs about you! Ha!

JON BOAT CHILI

1 tablespoon olive oil
1 pound skinless, boneless wild duck breast halves, cut into ½-inch cubes
1 onion, chopped
2 cloves garlic, chopped
2 cans Great Northern beans, rinsed and drained
1 can chicken broth
2 (4-ounce) cans chopped green chilis

1 teaspoon salt
1 teaspoon ground cumin
1 teaspoon dried oregano
½ teaspoon ground black pepper
¼ teaspoon cayenne pepper
1 cup sour cream
½ cup heavy whipping cream

Heat olive oil in a large saucepan or Dutch oven over medium heat; cook and stir wild duck meat, onion, and garlic into the hot oil until the duck is no longer pink in the center and the juices run clear, 10 to 15 minutes. Mix Great Northern beans, chicken broth, green chilis, salt, cumin, oregano, black pepper, and cayenne pepper into duck meat mixture; bring to a boil. Reduce heat, and simmer until flavors have blended, about 30 minutes. Remove chili from heat; stir in sour cream and whipping cream until well mixed. Check for seasonings, and serve with cornmeal bread or what we old Midwestern hunters call Johnny bread!

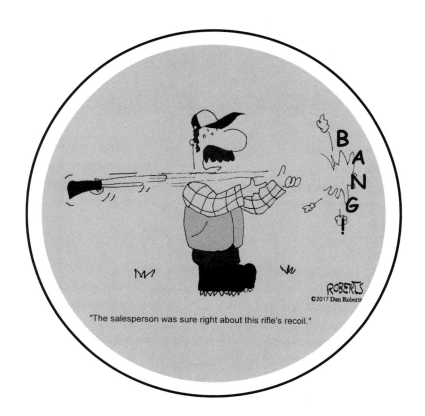

"The salesperson was sure right about this rifle's recoil."

Cooking with Grouse

AL SAUTNER'S PERFECT BIKER GROUSE

8 slices bacon

4 boneless grouse breast halves

Toothpicks

1 cup chicken broth

1 cup white wine

2 shallots, chopped

4 cloves garlic, chopped

1 teaspoon salt

Freshly ground black pepper to taste

3 tablespoons all-purpose flour

Preheat the oven to 325 degrees. Heat a large cast iron skillet over medium-high heat. Place the slices of bacon in the skillet, and fry until they have released their juices but are not yet crispy. Remove the bacon, and set aside. Place the grouse breast halves into the pan, and brown them quickly in the bacon fat, about 2 minutes per side. Remove the grouse pieces, and wrap each one with 2 slices of bacon. Secure with toothpicks. Pour enough of the drippings from the skillet into a baking dish to cover the bottom. Place the grouse pieces into the dish along with the chicken broth, white wine, shallots, garlic, salt, and black pepper. Roast uncovered for 45 minutes in the oven. Remove drippings from the baking dish using a turkey baster, and place in a saucepan. Whisk in the flour, and cook over medium-low heat, stirring constantly, until thickened. Serve with gravy. Al and Marge Sautner, who inspired this recipe, are two of the best friends a guy like me could be blessed with, and they keep South Carolina a fun place to hunt and fish. Cheers!

TAIL POINTER GROUSE

2 tablespoons butter

2 cloves garlic, sliced

2 (1-pound) grouse, cut into quarters and patted dry

¼ cup dry sherry or white wine

¼ cup chicken stock

2 teaspoons chopped fresh tarragon

¼ cup peach or apricot jam

1 teaspoon balsamic vinegar (or to taste)

Melt the butter with the garlic in a large iron skillet over low heat. Allow to bubble slowly for about 10 minutes to infuse the garlic into the butter, then remove garlic and reserve. Increase the heat to medium-high. When hot, cook the grouse until golden brown on both sides, about 3 minutes per side; then set aside. Pour the sherry into the skillet, and allow to simmer for 20 seconds. Stir in the chicken stock, tarragon, and jam; bring back to a simmer, then reduce heat to medium-low, cover, and simmer for 5 minutes. Add the balsamic vinegar, and cook covered for 2 minutes. Return the grouse to the pan, and simmer until fully cooked, 3 to 5 minutes.

TENDER GRILLED GROUSE

¼ cup Worcestershire sauce

2 tablespoons olive oil

½ teaspoon hot sauce

2 tablespoons minced garlic

¼ teaspoon black pepper

8 skinned, boned grouse breast halves

Stir together the Worcestershire sauce, olive oil, hot sauce, garlic, and pepper. Add the grouse breasts, and toss well to coat with the mixture. Cover, and marinate in the refrigerator for at least 30 minutes to overnight. Preheat a grill for medium-high heat. Grill the grouse breasts to desired doneness, about 5 minutes per side for medium-well, depending on the size of the breast and the temperature of the grill. This is an easy recipe and another great way to teach young hunters the art of outdoor cooking.

COUSIN RICK'S SIMPLE GROUSE

¼ cup shortening

6 grouse

Garlic powder to taste

Salt to taste

Ground black pepper to taste

1 cup all-purpose flour

¼ cup water

½ cup sour cream

Preheat oven to 350 degrees. Heat the shortening in a large, heavy-bottomed skillet over medium-high heat. Season the grouse with the garlic powder, salt, and pepper to taste. Place the flour in a shallow dish; roll the grouse in the flour. Working in batches, brown the grouse on all sides in the preheated shortening. Place the browned grouse in a large roasting pan or casserole dish; pour the water over the grouse, and cover with aluminum foil. Bake in oven for 1 hour, to an internal temperature of 165 degrees when measured from the thickest part of the thigh. Spoon the sour cream over the grouse, allowing the sour cream to melt before serving. This is another great, easy recipe for teaching young hunters about cooking.

CORN FINGER GROUSE

¼ cup ground pork

2 tablespoons chopped fresh parsley

2 tablespoons finely chopped carrots

2 tablespoons finely chopped celery

1 clove fresh garlic, chopped

2½ tablespoons fresh bread crumbs

Ground black pepper to taste

8 grouse, cleaned and split lengthwise

1 tablespoon bacon drippings

Preheat the oven broiler. In a bowl, mix the pork, parsley, carrots, celery, garlic, bread crumbs, and pepper. Arrange the grouse in a baking dish. Separate the skin from the breast of each grouse, and stuff with equal amounts of the stuffing mixture. Brush with bacon drippings. Broil the grouse about 7 minutes on each side in oven, to a minimum internal temperature of 180 degrees. Check for seasonings, and serve.

SAVORY ROASTED GROUSE

2 tablespoons olive oil, divided

½ teaspoon cumin

¼ teaspoon ground coriander

4 whole grouse

8 slices cured lemon, patted dry

1 pinch cayenne pepper (optional)

1 cup chicken broth

1 slice cured lemon, minced

Salt to taste

Freshly ground black pepper to taste

Preheat oven to 425 degrees. Whisk 1 tablespoon olive oil, cumin, and coriander together in a large bowl; place grouse in bowl, and toss to coat completely. Place 1 cured lemon slice in the cavity of each grouse. Tie a piece of twine around the wings and under the breast above the legs of each grouse; also tie the legs together with twine. Heat remaining 1 tablespoon olive oil in a large skillet over high heat. Cook grouse in hot oil until browned on all sides, 2 to 4 minutes per side. Remove from heat. Turn each grouse, so that the breast side is facing up. Place 1 slice cured lemon on each breast, and sprinkle each with cayenne pepper if desired. Roast in oven until slightly pink at the bone, 10 to 15 minutes. Remove grouse to a plate. Pour chicken broth into skillet, and bring to a boil while scraping the browned bits off the bottom of the skillet with a wooden spoon. Cook until reduced by half, about 5 minutes. Stir minced lemon into broth mixture. Return grouse to skillet, and pour sauce over grouse until heated through, 2 to 3 minutes, then season with salt and pepper to taste.

Cooking with Quail

CARLSON'S HAWKEYE QUAIL

¼ cup shortening
8 quail
Garlic powder to taste
Salt to taste

Ground black pepper to taste
1 cup all-purpose flour
¼ cup water
½ cup sour cream

Preheat oven to 350 degrees. Heat the shortening in a large, heavy-bottomed skillet over medium-high heat. Season the quail with the garlic powder, salt, and pepper to taste. Place the flour in a shallow dish; roll the quail in the flour. Working in batches, brown the quail on all sides in the preheated shortening. Place the browned quail in a large roasting pan or casserole dish; pour the water over the quail, and cover with aluminum foil. Bake in oven for 1 hour, to an internal temperature of 165 degrees when measured from the thickest part of the thigh. Spoon the sour cream over the quail, allowing the sour cream to melt before serving.

HOUSINDA QUAIL

¼ cup ground pork
2 tablespoons chopped fresh parsley
2 tablespoons finely chopped carrots
2 tablespoons finely chopped celery
1 clove fresh garlic, chopped

2½ tablespoons fresh bread crumbs
Ground black pepper to taste
8 quail, cleaned and split lengthwise
1 tablespoon bacon drippings

Preheat the oven broiler. In a bowl, mix the pork, parsley, carrots, celery, garlic, bread crumbs, and pepper. Arrange the quail in a baking dish. Separate the skin from the breast of each quail, and stuff with equal amounts of the stuffing mixture. Brush with bacon drippings. Broil the quail 7 minutes on each side in oven, to a minimum internal temperature of 180 degrees.

GEODE RANCH HAND QUAIL

2 tablespoons olive oil, divided
½ teaspoon cumin
¼ teaspoon ground coriander
4 whole quail
8 slices cured lemon, patted dry

¼ teaspoon cayenne pepper
1 cup chicken broth
1 slice cured lemon, minced
Salt to taste
Freshly ground black pepper to taste

Preheat oven to 425 degrees. Whisk 1 tablespoon olive oil, cumin, and coriander together in a large bowl; place quail in bowl, and toss to coat quail completely. Place 1 cured lemon slice in the cavity of each quail. Tie a piece of twine around the wings and under breast above the legs of each quail; tie legs together with twine. Heat remaining 1 tablespoon olive oil in a large skillet over high heat. Cook quail in hot oil until browned on all sides, 2 to 4 minutes per side. Remove from heat. Turn each quail so that the breast side is facing up. Place 1 slice cured lemon on each quail breast and sprinkle each with cayenne pepper. Roast in oven until slightly pink at the bone, 10 to 15 minutes. Remove quail to a plate. Pour chicken broth into skillet and bring to a boil while scraping the browned bits off the bottom of the skillet with a wooden spoon. Cook until reduced by half, about 5 minutes. Stir minced lemon into broth mixture. Return quail to skillet and pour sauce over quail until heated through, 2 to 3 minutes, then season with salt and pepper to taste.

GRELK FARMS QUAIL SOUP

3 pounds quail or pheasant meat
2 parsnips, peeled and chopped
1 medium head garlic, peeled
2 large onions, chopped
5 carrots, chopped
2 zucchini, chopped
½ cup chopped fresh parsley
2 stalks celery, chopped
2 potatoes, peeled and chopped

1 sweet potato, peeled and cubed
1 packet chicken vegetable soup mix
1 tablespoon dried oregano
1 teaspoon paprika
8 cups water
½ bottle white wine
Salt to taste
Ground black pepper to taste

In a large soup pot or Dutch oven, combine all ingredients. Cover, and bring to a boil over high heat. Boil 30 minutes, partially covered, then reduce heat to low and simmer another 90 minutes. Check the quail soup for seasonings, and serve hot with fresh bread. Good stuff!

HUNGRY HUNTERS QUAIL'S NEST
(QUAIL AND BISCUITS)

¼ cup butter

2 cloves garlic, minced

½ cup chopped onion

½ cup chopped celery

½ cup chopped baby carrots

½ cup all-purpose flour

2 teaspoons sugar

1 teaspoon salt

3 teaspoons dried basil, divided

½ teaspoon ground black pepper

4 cups chicken broth

1 (10-ounce) can peas, drained

4 cups diced cooked quail breast

2 cups buttermilk baking mix

⅔ cup milk

Preheat oven to 350 degrees. Lightly grease a 9- by 13-inch baking dish. In a skillet, melt the butter over medium-high heat. Cook and stir the garlic, onion, celery, and carrots in butter until tender. Mix in the flour, sugar, salt, 1 teaspoon dried basil, and pepper. Stir in broth, and bring to a boil. Keep stirring constantly while it boils for 1 minute, then reduce heat and stir in peas. Simmer 5 minutes, then mix in quail breast meat. Transfer mixture to the prepared baking dish. In a medium bowl, combine the baking mix and remaining 2 teaspoons dried basil. Stir in milk to form a dough. Divide the dough into 6 to 8 balls. On floured wax paper, use your palm to flatten each ball of dough into a circular shape; place on top of quail meat mixture. Bake in oven for 30 minutes. Cover with foil, and bake for 10 more minutes. To serve, spoon quail mixture over biscuits.

EASY CORNBREAD QUAIL PIE

1 can cream of chicken soup

1 can whole kernel corn, drained

2 cups cubed cooked quail or pheasant meat

1 package corn muffin mix

¾ cup milk

1 egg

½ cup shredded cheddar cheese

Heat the oven to 400 degrees. Stir the soup, corn, and quail meat in a 9-inch pie plate. Stir the muffin mix, milk, and egg in a small bowl until just blended. Spread the batter into the pie plate over the game bird mixture. Bake for 30 minutes or until the topping is golden brown. Sprinkle with the cheese. Let stand until the cheese is melted. Check for seasonings, and serve hot.

CHAPTER 7

Wild Game Cooking for a Crowd

If you like large hunting groups, you'll love these big wild game feast recipes. As a rule of thumb, if you are serving fish as a main course, estimate about 6 ounces per guest. Servings for other types of meat will vary. An 18-pound wild turkey, a 12-pound elk/venison roast, or a 7-pound boneless boar roast will be enough for 25 to 30 people. For even larger groups, just double or triple the recipe as needed. For example, for 60 people, you'd want a 24-pound venison roast.

BUCK EVE SLOPPY DOE'S

8 pounds deer burger

3 cups diced celery

3 cups diced onion

½ cup flour

¾ cup mustard

¾ cup vinegar

¾ cup brown sugar

2 bottles ketchup

3 cups beef stock

Tomato juice (optional)

80 hamburger buns

Brown deer meat, celery, and onion in a large Dutch oven. Stir in flour slowly. Add remaining ingredients, and simmer. If the mixture seems dry, or needs a little punch of flavor, I add tomato juice. Check for seasonings, and serve on buns. Feeds about 80 people.

HUNTERS' CABIN KITCHEN GAMEBALLS & PASTA

GAMEBALLS (MEATBALLS):

3 slices white bread, torn into pieces

¼ cup milk

2 pounds deer burger or elk burger

2 eggs

½ cup grated Romano cheese

1 pinch dried parsley

¾ teaspoon salt (or to taste)

¼ teaspoon ground black pepper (or to taste)

SAUCE:

3 tablespoons olive oil

4 onions, chopped

6 cloves garlic, chopped

12 links sweet Italian sausage

2 pounds cubed venison brisket

½ pound pork neck bones

4 cans tomato paste

3 cans crushed tomatoes

½ cup red wine

4 bay leaves

¼ teaspoon ground cinnamon

¼ teaspoon dried parsley

1 teaspoon dried basil

Seasoned salt to taste

Ground black pepper to taste

3 (16-ounce) packages dry pasta

To make the gameballs, combine bread and milk in a medium bowl. Mix in ground venison, eggs, Romano cheese, parsley, and salt and pepper to taste. Form golf ball–sized meatballs, and place them in the freezer to firm up for at least 45 minutes to an hour. To make the sauce, heat olive oil in a large iron pot on medium heat; stir in onions. Cook and stir until the onions have softened and turned translucent, about 5 minutes. Add garlic and sausage links; cook about 3 minutes more. Meanwhile, in a large skillet over medium heat, brown venison chunks and pork neck bones; set aside. When onions and garlic are done, turn heat down to low. Add tomato paste, and cook for a few minutes. Stir in the browned venison and pork, crushed tomatoes, wine, bay leaves, cinnamon, parsley, basil, and salt and pepper. Bring sauce to a simmer, then reduce the heat to low, and cook for 3 to 4 hours. Add the meatballs and let sauce simmer for 1 hour. When sauce is nearly ready, bring a large pot of lightly salted water to a boil. Add pasta, and cook for 8 to 10 minutes or until al dente; drain. Cover pasta with sauce and meatballs, and serve immediately. This recipe is just as great if you substitute bear or boar. Feeds about 20 people.

"I'M EXPECTING A LARGE CROWD FOR SUPPER."

BUCK-IN-RUT SKEWERS

1½ cups light brown sugar
1 cup soy sauce
½ cup pineapple juice
1 cup dark beer

¼ cup vegetable oil
3 large garlic cloves, chopped
5 pounds boneless venison steak, cut into ¼-inch slices
Bamboo skewers, soaked in water

Whisk brown sugar, soy sauce, pineapple juice, beer, vegetable oil, and garlic together in a large bowl; drop deer slices into the mixture, and stir to coat. Cover bowl with plastic wrap. Marinate the deer meat in refrigerator for 24 hours. Remove deer from the marinade, shaking to remove any excess liquid, and discard the marinade. Preheat grill for medium heat, and lightly oil the grate. Thread deer slices in a zigzag onto the skewers, then cook skewers on preheated grill until venison is cooked through, about 3 minutes per side. This is an easy recipe to double or even triple for your next wild game feast. Feeds about 20 hungry, hungry hunters.

MILL DAM ROAD LOOSE GAME BBQ

8 pounds boneless game roast (elk/deer/bear)
2 cups beer (or substitute chicken stock)
3 tablespoons white vinegar
4 tablespoons brown sugar
2 teaspoons dry mustard
4 tablespoons Worcestershire sauce

3 cups ketchup
2 teaspoons salt
¾ teaspoon ground black pepper
¼ teaspoon cayenne pepper
6 cloves garlic, minced

Place the game roast into a slow cooker along with the beer. Cover, and cook on low for 4 to 6 hours, until game meat can be easily shredded with a fork. Shred the game meat, removing fat as you go. Remove ½ cup of the broth from the slow cooker, and reserve for later. Add the vinegar, brown sugar, dry mustard, Worcestershire sauce, and ketchup. Mix in the salt, pepper, cayenne, and garlic. Stir until the game meat is well coated. Cover, and continue to cook game meat on low for an additional 4 to 6 hours. Add the reserved broth only if necessary to maintain moisture. Check for seasonings, and serve on toasted buns. If you like, the meat can be frozen for future wild game feeds. Feeds about 25.

GAME FEED HUNTERS DEER SUMMER SAUSAGE

5 pounds ground venison

2 tablespoons sugar-based curing mixture

2 teaspoons mustard seed

2½ teaspoons garlic salt

2½ teaspoons ground black pepper

1 teaspoon liquid smoke flavoring

Place the venison in a large mixing bowl. Sprinkle with the curing mixture, mustard seed, garlic salt, pepper, and liquid smoke. Mix well with your hands until evenly blended and mixture begins to stick together, about 2 minutes. Cover the bowl with plastic wrap, and refrigerate for 3 days, mixing well each day. Preheat an oven to 200 degrees. Divide the mixture into five 1-pound logs, place logs onto a broiler pan, and then cover with a sheet of aluminum foil. Bake in oven until the logs are no longer pink in the center and an instant-read thermometer inserted into the center reads 160 degrees, 6 to 8 hours. Turn the meat once or twice during cooking. Allow to cool before slicing thinly and serving.

BRAISED BOAR AND SAUERKRAUT FEAST

4 cans sauerkraut (drained), divided

6 pounds wild boar roast

2 large onions, quartered

8 potatoes, peeled and cubed

8 carrots, cut into 2-inch pieces

2 cans or bottles of beer

Preheat the oven to 300 degrees. Pour two cans of sauerkraut into the bottom of a Dutch oven. Set the roast on top of it, then arrange the onions, potatoes, and carrots around the roast. Cover with the remaining cans of sauerkraut, and pour in the beer. Cover with a lid. Bake in oven until the roast is extremely tender, about 3 hours. Check for seasonings, and serve to the hungry hunters! Feeds about 15.

"So this is why you shouldn't grill out on Trick-or-Treat Night."

HUNTERS' LODGE BISON

BISON ROAST:

2 tablespoons olive oil

1 (6-pound) bison tenderloin roast

2 teaspoons kosher salt

2 teaspoons dried thyme

1 teaspoon coarsely ground black pepper

CHERRY-ONION CHUTNEY:

2 tablespoons olive oil

3 cups chopped onion

1 cup packed brown sugar

½ cup balsamic vinegar

1 teaspoon ground cinnamon

½ teaspoon ground cloves

Cayenne pepper to taste

6 cups frozen tart red-pitted cherries

2 medium pears, cored and chopped

Salt to taste

Ground black pepper to taste

Preheat oven to 425 degrees. Brush 2 tablespoons oil over bison tenderloin roast. For the rub, in a small bowl stir together salt, thyme, and coarsely ground black pepper. Sprinkle mixture evenly over bison tenderloin; rub in with your fingers. Place tenderloin on a rack set in a shallow roasting pan. Insert an oven-ready meat thermometer into center of the bison tenderloin. Roast, uncovered, for 1 hour 10 minutes or until meat thermometer registers 135 degrees for medium-rare. (For medium, roast for 1 hour 45 minutes or until meat thermometer registers 150 degrees.) Transfer bison tenderloin to a cutting board, and cover with foil; let stand for 15 minutes. Temperature of the bison tenderloin after standing should be 160 degrees for medium. Slice tenderloin across the grain, and arrange on a serving platter. Meanwhile, while the bison is in the oven, begin on the cherry-onion chutney. Heat 2 tablespoons oil over medium-high heat in a large iron skillet. Cook onions in hot oil for 8 to 10 minutes or until golden brown. Remove onions from skillet; set aside. Add brown sugar, vinegar, cinnamon, cloves, and cayenne pepper to skillet. Bring to boiling; reduce heat. Add cherries. Simmer, uncovered, for about 15 minutes. Add pears, and cook for 5 more minutes or until pears are softened. Stir in cooked onion. Season to taste with salt and black pepper. This recipe is always a big hit at the game feeds I host! I have also used bear and venison meat with this recipe. Feeds about 20.

BUTTON BUCK NOODLES

2 cans condensed cream of celery soup

2 cans condensed French onion soup

1 (16-ounce) container sour cream

6 pounds precooked/seasoned deer burger meatballs
(see recipe on page 157)

2 (16-ounce) packages uncooked egg noodles

½ cup butter

In a large slow cooker, mix together the cream of celery soup, French onion soup, and sour cream. Stir in the cooked deer meatballs. Cook on high heat for 3 to 4 hours. Bring a large pot of lightly salted water to a boil. Add pasta, and cook for 8 to 10 minutes or until al dente; drain. In a large bowl, toss the pasta with butter. Serve deer meatballs and sauce over the cooked pasta. Feeds about 15.

DES MOINES COUNTY PHEASANT FOR EVER-SPICED VENISON MEATBALLS

MEATBALLS:

4 eggs, beaten

½ cup vodka

½ cup water

1 tablespoon Worcestershire sauce

2 tablespoons dried minced onion flakes

1 teaspoon garlic powder (or to taste)

½ teaspoon salt (or to taste)

½ teaspoon ground black pepper (or to taste)

4 pounds deer burger

2 pounds ground turkey (preferably wild turkey, if you still have some in the freezer)

1 (15-ounce) package Italian seasoned bread crumbs

SAUCE:

2 (28-ounce) cans crushed tomatoes

2 (14.25-ounce) cans tomato purée

1 (18-ounce) bottle hickory smoke–flavored barbecue sauce

1 can crushed pineapple

1 cup brown sugar

1 (14-ounce) bottle ketchup

½ cup vodka

2 tablespoons dried minced onion flakes

1 teaspoon garlic powder (or to taste)

½ teaspoon salt (or to taste)

½ teaspoon ground black pepper (or to taste)

In a large bowl, combine eggs, ½ cup vodka, and Worcestershire sauce. Season with 2 tablespoons onion flakes, garlic powder, salt, and pepper. Mix in deer burger, ground turkey, and bread crumbs. Shape into meatballs, and set aside. In a very large pot over medium heat, begin the sauce by combining crushed tomatoes, tomato purée, barbecue sauce, pineapple, brown sugar, ketchup, ½ cup vodka, and water. Season to taste with onion flakes, garlic powder, salt, and pepper. Bring to a boil, reduce heat, and let simmer. Heat a large, heavy skillet over medium heat. Cook meatballs until evenly brown on all sides. Carefully place into sauce, and simmer for at least an hour. Check for seasonings, and serve hot. This is a crowd pleaser!

CAMP COMMANDER VENISON SOUP

3 pounds ground elk or buffalo

1 cup diced onion

2 garlic cloves, chopped

2 bay leaves

6 beef bouillon cubes

4 cups diced potatoes

2 cups corn

2 quarts water

2 quarts canned tomatoes (or just juice if you prefer)

1 tablespoon sugar

1 tablespoon salt

¼ teaspoon pepper

2 cups diced celery

2 large carrots, sliced

1 can red kidney beans

2 cups shredded cabbage

Any other vegetables you like!

Brown meat in a large Dutch oven or large pot. Stir in onions and garlic; brown 5 minutes more. Add remaining ingredients, and simmer 2 hours. Adjust seasonings to taste. Add any other vegetables you wish, like zucchini, green pepper, green beans, or peas. Makes around 2 gallons of great tasting soup, which will feed about 30 hunters!

SPARKY SPARKS MOUNTAIN MAN ELK CHILI

3 pounds ground elk or venison

2 (28-ounce) cans diced tomatoes, juice reserved

4 (16-ounce) cans kidney beans (or substitute black or pinto beans), rinsed and drained

1 pound smoked kielbasa, halved and sliced

2 large onions, halved and thinly sliced

2 (8-ounces) cans tomato sauce

⅔ cup hickory-flavored barbecue sauce

1½ cups water

½ cup packed brown sugar

5 fresh banana peppers, seeded and sliced

2 tablespoons chili powder

2 teaspoons ground mustard

2 teaspoons instant coffee granules

1 teaspoon dried oregano

1 teaspoon dried thyme

1 teaspoon sage

½ to 1 teaspoon cayenne pepper

½ to 1 teaspoon crushed red pepper flakes

2 garlic cloves, minced

In a large kettle or Dutch oven, cook elk over medium heat until no longer pink; drain. Stir in the remaining ingredients, and then bring to a boil. Reduce heat, cover, and simmer for 1 hour, stirring occasionally. Check at the end for seasonings, and serve with cornbread. This is a very good-tasting chili. It feeds 25, although to feed 50, just double the recipe. Yes, it's that easy!

CHAPTER 8

Wild Game Cooking with Beer

I love my job! Nothing goes together quite like beer and wild game, and here are a few reasons why:

- First and foremost, beer can impart interesting new flavors to dishes—bitterness from the hops and/or sweetness from the malt.
- Enzymes in beer have a tenderizing effect, which makes it a valuable ingredient in marinades.
- Beer is versatile and can be used in a whole range of cooking techniques, including baking, braising, batter-frying, deglazing, marinades, poaching, and simmering, as well as making sauces and salad dressings. I have read of folks steaming their shellfish—and even hotdogs—over beer!

I am not trying to say that beer is ideal for every wild game dish—some ingredients just don't mix well with beer. It is important not to allow the flavor of the beer to overwhelm the other ingredients.

While a glass of beer is often a great accompaniment to a meal, you don't need to serve the same beer you used in a recipe with the finished dish. Sometimes using the same beer can complement the wild game flavor, but on other occasions, you may prefer a contrast.

Of course, the best way to figure out how to use beer as an ingredient is to try it out yourself and see what works. My hunting buddies and I are convinced that if you try some of the recipes here, perhaps with your own adaptations, you will come to value beer as a versatile companion in the camp kitchen—and at the very least, the occasional mouthful will be refreshing while you're slaving over a Dutch oven!

A Few Rules of Thumb

- Beer is by nature bitter, which comes from the hops, although malt adds a sweet flavor that counteracts and harmonizes with the bitterness. The balance between these elements will define the character of a beer, and this is why different beers used in the same recipe can produce very different results.

- Sweet foods can profit from being offset by the hops' bitter taste. These foods include sugary vegetables like onions, carrots, and sweet corn or even honey, molasses, and sugar. Caramelized onions are a classic example of a sweet vegetable that matches perfectly with beer. (Just imagine a homemade deer burger, smothered in caramelized onions, accompanied by a nice pint of bitter—a hunter's bliss!)

- The bitter hop flavor also helps counteract the richness of creamy, oil-based, or cheesy dishes, but use beer as sparingly as you would a squeeze of lime or add a touch of vinegar. Always add the beer very gradually, tasting as you go—it's easy to add more, but very difficult to take some out!

- Acidic foods like tomatoes, citrus fruits, vinegar, and mustard can complement the sweet malt flavors of beer, adding balance and depth to the dish.

- The yeast in bottle-conditioned beers lends itself to baking and battering. Breads, fritters, and pancakes all profit from being made with yeasty brews, which lighten the texture and make for tender, tasty crusts. Baked goods using beer generally have a moister texture and a longer shelf life. In batter coatings for fried foods, the yeast in the beer acts as a mild leavening agent, causing the batter to puff up, as well as enhances the flavor.

- Beer has wonderful tenderizing properties, making it an excellent choice for a game marinade. You can save money by buying cheaper, tougher cuts of game meat, and they will still make an impressive dish if you marinate them well.

- Game combines well with beer, but so does fowl and fish. If you are hesitant about beer cooking, start by simply marinating different meats or fish in a variety of beers—it's a great way to learn about the range of flavors at your disposal.

- The more the beer is cooked and reduced, the stronger its flavor will be. If the dish requires long cooking and reduction, be careful about using a beer that's too strongly flavored or too bitter, as it might end up overwhelming the dish. A useful technique is to start off with a small amount of the beer, with the rest of the liquid made up of the appropriate stock. Then, you can add more of the beer later in the cooking process, which ensures it will provide a subtler flavor.

- If you're cooking a savory game stew with beer and it tastes too bitter, you can always remedy that with some puréed, sautéed carrots, a few drops of lemon juice, and extra spices (such as rosemary or thyme).

- If you're making a sauce with onions or mushrooms and the beer turns the flavor too bitter, add a splash of sweet Madeira or sherry to round it out.

- When you're going to add beer to a mixture, use a larger-than-usual mixing bowl—bottled beer is likely to foam up on contact with other food ingredients! If that causes problems, you could try whisking your beer in a separate bowl to release some of the excess carbonation, and let it settle before measuring into your recipe.

Thickening Dishes With Beer

When you cook with beer, you are adding liquid to your recipe. This can lead to a dilemma: how do you get those extra flavors without ending up with a runny mess? The answer is to have a range of thickening techniques at your disposal.

When making a soup or stew, adding too much beer at the beginning can make the stew watery. Worse still, if you try to boil off the liquid to reduce the stew volume, the flavor is likely to become too bitter. But there is a solution—just stir in a few handfuls of dried potato flakes or take a small amount of the watery broth, mix it with corn flour, then stir that mixture back into the stew pot. Keep stirring for a few minutes while simmering gently, and it will thicken up nicely.

Does the Beer Keep Its Alcohol?

Many people think that cooking destroys the alcohol content of the beer (or wine) you use, but this is not necessarily true. It is true that alcohol is sensitive to heat, and that the longer you cook a dish and the higher the temperature, the smaller the amount of alcohol that will remain in the finished dish.

WILD IRISH VENISON STEW

2 tablespoons olive oil	½ teaspoon ground black pepper (plus more for seasoning)
1 onion, chopped	2 pounds venison stew meat, cubed
3 cloves garlic, minced	3 cups stout beer
1 teaspoon salt (plus more for seasoning)	4 potatoes (2 peeled and sliced, 2 peeled and quartered)

Heat the olive oil in a large pot over medium heat. Stir in the onion, garlic, salt, and pepper. Cook and stir until the onion has softened and turned translucent, about 5 minutes. Stir in the venison, beer, sliced potatoes, and quartered potatoes. Bring to a boil over high heat, then reduce heat to medium-low, cover, and simmer until the venison is tender, about 2 hours. Season to taste with more salt and pepper, and serve.

AUGUSTA TAP BEER BATTER CATFISH

4 cups pastry flour

1 tablespoon baking powder

½ teaspoon baking soda

2 tablespoons cornstarch

3 eggs

1½ cups milk

¾ cup beer

Salt to taste

Ground black pepper to taste

⅛ teaspoon garlic powder

2 quarts vegetable oil for frying

1½ pounds catfish fillets

In a medium bowl, stir together flour, baking powder, baking soda, and cornstarch. In a large bowl, beat together eggs and milk. Mix in beer with the eggs and milk, then stir in flour mixture. Season with salt, black pepper, and garlic powder. In an electric deep fryer or a heavy saucepan, heat oil to 375 degrees. Coat the catfish in batter, and submerge in hot oil. Fry until golden brown, about 4 to 5 minutes, and then serve.

SPARKY SPARK'S BUFFALO IN THE SUDS STEAKS

2 buffalo steaks

¼ cup dark beer

2 tablespoons teriyaki sauce

2 tablespoons brown sugar

½ teaspoon seasoned salt, divided

½ teaspoon black pepper, divided

½ teaspoon garlic powder, divided

Preheat grill for high heat. Use a fork to poke holes all over the surface of the buffalo steaks, and place steaks in a large baking dish. In a bowl, mix together beer, teriyaki sauce, and brown sugar. Pour sauce over buffalo steaks, and let sit about 5 minutes. Sprinkle with ¼ teaspoon of the seasoned salt, pepper, and garlic powder; set aside for 10 minutes. Turn buffalo steaks over, sprinkle with remaining ¼ teaspoon seasoned salt, pepper, and garlic powder, and continue marinating for 10 more minutes. Remove steaks from marinade. Pour marinade into a small saucepan, bring to a boil, and cook for several minutes. Lightly oil the grill grate. Grill steaks for 7 minutes per side, or to desired doneness. During the last few minutes of grilling, baste the buffalo steaks with boiled marinade to enhance the flavor and ensure juiciness.

RAZORBACK BREW CHOPS

2 cups ketchup
¾ cup packed brown sugar

1 (12-fluid ounce) can or bottle beer
8 nice-sized boar chops

Preheat oven to 350 degrees. In a medium bowl, combine the ketchup, brown sugar, and beer. Mix well, and pour into a 9- by 13-inch baking dish. Place the boar chops over this mixture in the dish. Bake uncovered for 1 hour, until internal boar meat temperature reaches 150 degrees. (Try placing foil over the boar chops if they start to brown too quickly.) This is an easy and tasty way to cook your boar!

BEER BAKED BEAR ROAST

2 tablespoons vegetable oil
1 tablespoon mustard
2 tablespoons caraway seeds
1 tablespoon garlic powder
1 tablespoon salt
2 teaspoons ground black pepper

5 pounds bear roast
3 medium onions, chopped
½ cup beer
2 tablespoons butter
1 tablespoon cornstarch

In a bowl, form a paste using the vegetable oil, mustard, caraway seeds, garlic powder, salt, and pepper. Rub over the bear roast, and let sit about 30 minutes. Meanwhile, preheat oven to 350 degrees. Arrange the onions in the bottom of a large roasting pan, and then pour in the beer. Place the bear roast, fat-side down, on top of the onions. Cover the pan with foil. Roast 1 hour in oven. Remove foil, turn roast, and score the fat. Continue roasting 2½ hours, to a minimum internal temperature of 145 degrees. Remove from heat, reserving pan juices, and let sit about 20 minutes before slicing thinly. In a saucepan, bring the reserved pan juices to a boil. Mix in the butter and cornstarch to thicken, reduce heat, and simmer 5 to 10 minutes. Serve with the sliced bear. This is a very good recipe to use for that big old bear roast, with a flavor that's just outstanding! This recipe has been in my family for three generations.

BEER CURRIED DUCK BREAST

4 to 6 medium-size duck breast halves
2 tablespoons butter
1 onion, chopped
⅔ cup beer
1 (10.75-ounce) can condensed tomato soup

1 teaspoon curry powder
½ teaspoon dried basil
½ teaspoon ground black pepper
¼ cup grated Parmesan cheese

Preheat oven to 350 degrees. Place duck in a 9- by 13-inch baking dish. Melt butter in a cast iron skillet over medium heat. Sauté onion, then stir in beer, soup, curry powder, basil, and pepper. Reduce heat to low, and simmer for about 10 minutes, then pour over duck. Bake at 350 degrees for 1 hour; sprinkle with cheese for last 10 minutes of baking.

SAVORY SHREDDED BIG GAME ROAST

5 pounds your choice of big game roast
(works great with all!)
3 cloves garlic, cut in slivers
1 tablespoon paprika
1 tablespoon celery salt
1 tablespoon garlic powder
1 tablespoon dried parsley
½ tablespoon ground black pepper
½ tablespoon chili powder
½ tablespoon cayenne pepper

½ teaspoon seasoned salt
½ teaspoon mustard powder
½ teaspoon dried tarragon
½ cup beer
1½ tablespoons Worcestershire sauce
4 tablespoons hot pepper sauce
2 teaspoons liquid smoke flavoring
1 large onion, chopped
1 green bell pepper, chopped
2 jalapeño chili peppers, chopped

Using a sharp knife, poke several 1-inch deep holes into the big game roast. Insert the garlic slivers into the holes. In a small bowl, combine the paprika, celery salt, garlic powder, parsley, ground black pepper, chili powder, cayenne pepper, seasoned salt, mustard powder, and dried tarragon; mix together well, and rub over the meat. In a separate small bowl, combine the beer, Worcestershire sauce, hot pepper sauce, and liquid smoke. Mix well. Place the roast in a slow cooker, and pour this mixture over the game meat. Add the onion, bell pepper, and jalapeño chili peppers to the slow cooker, and then cook on low for 10 hours (or more, if desired). Check for seasonings, and serve.

COONS IN THE BEER STEW

3 pounds raccoon meat, cut into 2-inch cubes
Salt to taste
Ground black pepper to taste
1 tablespoon vegetable oil
1 tablespoon butter
1 large onion, chopped
2 cloves garlic, minced
1 tablespoon all-purpose flour
1 bay leaf
¾ teaspoon caraway seed

1 (12-ounce) bottle dark beer
2 cups chicken broth
3 carrots, cut into 1-inch pieces
2 stalks celery, cut into 1-inch pieces
¼ cup chopped fresh flat-leaf parsley (plus another tablespoon or so for seasoning)
3 tablespoons balsamic vinegar
12 Brussels sprouts, halved
3 cups mashed potatoes (or as needed)

Season the raccoon cubes with salt and black pepper. Heat vegetable oil in a pot over high heat. Working in batches, cook and stir raccoon in hot oil until browned on all sides, 5 to 10 minutes. Transfer raccoon to a bowl, and reduce heat to medium. Melt butter in the pot. Cook and stir onion with a pinch of salt in hot butter until onion is softened and translucent, 7 to 10 minutes. Add garlic; sauté until fragrant, about 30 seconds. Stir flour into onion mixture; cook and stir until flour is completely incorporated, about 2 minutes. Add bay leaf and caraway seed; cook for 2 minutes more. Pour beer into onion mixture. Cook and stir until thickened, 1 to 3 minutes. Stir raccoon, chicken broth, carrots, and celery into beer mixture, then bring to simmer. Stir ¼ cup parsley and balsamic vinegar into stew, reduce heat to medium-low, and simmer until coon meat is fork-tender, about 2 hours. Bring a large pot of lightly salted water to a boil. Add the Brussels sprouts, and cook uncovered until almost tender, about 5 minutes; drain. Stir Brussels sprouts into stew, and simmer until heated through, about 5 minutes. Season with salt and pepper to taste. Divide mashed potatoes between 6 bowls. Ladle stew over potatoes, top each with a pinch of parsley, and serve. This tasty coon will be a hit at your next wild game feed!

"Ah! Just the right amount of tabasco sauce and chili peppers!"

ELK/DEER HUNTER'S CABIN PIE

3 tablespoons olive oil, divided

1 pound venison stew meat, cubed

2 slices bacon, chopped

1 white onion, chopped

1 carrot, sliced

1/3 pound mushrooms, sliced

1 clove garlic, crushed

1 teaspoon sugar

1½ tablespoons all-purpose flour

1 cup Irish stout beer

1¼ cups beef stock

½ teaspoon ground thyme

2 bay leaves

½ teaspoon cornstarch (or as needed)

1 teaspoon water

1 sheet frozen puff pastry, thawed

1 egg, beaten

Heat 2 tablespoons of olive oil in a large pot over medium heat, and brown the venison stew meat on all sides, about 10 minutes; set aside. Heat the remaining 1 tablespoon of olive oil, and cook the bacon until it just begins to brown. Stir in the onion, carrot, mushrooms, garlic, and sugar. Cook the vegetables until soft and browned, 10 to 15 minutes. Stir in the flour until smoothly mixed, and gradually add the beer and beef stock. Mix in the thyme and bay leaves, as well as the reserved cooked venison. Cover, and bring the mixture to a boil. Reduce heat to a simmer until the venison meat is tender, stirring occasionally, about 1 hour and 15 minutes. Remove the cover, turn the heat up to medium, and let the stew boil until slightly thickened, about 15 more minutes. Mix cornstarch with water, and stir into the stew; let simmer for 30 more minutes to blend flavors. Remove from heat, and discard bay leaves. Preheat oven to 350 degrees. Spread the filling into a 9-inch pie dish, and then trim the puff pastry into a 10-inch circle to place on top of the filling. Pinch and crimp the edges of the pastry with a fork, sealing it to the dish, then cut 2 steam vents into the pastry with a sharp knife. Brush the top of the pie with beaten egg. Bake in oven until the crust is browned, 30 to 40 minutes. Check for seasonings, and serve.

BUCK, BEANS, AND BEER CAMP CHILI

1 tablespoon vegetable oil

1 onion, diced

2 pounds deer burger

2 teaspoons salt (plus more to taste)

3 cloves garlic, minced

3 tablespoons ground ancho chili powder

1 tablespoon ground cumin

1 teaspoon paprika

1 teaspoon ground black pepper

$1/8$ teaspoon ground cinnamon

1 (12-ounce) bottle beer

1 teaspoon unsweetened cocoa powder

¼ teaspoon dried oregano

¼ teaspoon ground cayenne pepper

2 cups water (or as needed)

1 cup tomato purée

$2/3$ cup diced poblano pepper

2 (12-ounce) cans pinto beans, drained and rinsed well

Place a pot over high heat. Drizzle in vegetable oil. Add diced onion, deer burger, and salt. Use a wooden spoon to break up meat into small pieces as it browns. After meat browns and releases its juices, continue stirring until the juices evaporate, about 4 minutes. Reduce heat to medium-high. Add garlic, chili powder, cumin, paprika, black pepper, and cinnamon. Cook and stir until mixture begins to darken, 3 or 4 minutes, then stir in beer. After the beer, add cocoa powder, oregano, cayenne, water, and tomato purée; stir well. Adjust heat to medium-low and bring to a simmer for 30 minutes. Stir in poblano pepper and pinto beans. If mixture becomes too thick, add a bit more water. Simmer until peppers are tender and flavors have blended, about 30 more minutes, and then serve.

"Yah, I think it looks like Cousin Rick's work too."

THE CRITICAL STEPS TO GAME MEAT FLAVOR

I can't tell you how many times I have heard that wild game—such as venison—has a bad or gamey taste. I know wild game is great-tasting, and venison is among the best-flavored meats a person can eat. Venison was the meat of kings and queens for a reason: IT'S GOOD! So, in closing I have listed tips and recommendations on how to keep the wonderful meat you have harvested tasting delicious. I'm going to focus on venison, but this advice applies to all game. Deer just happens to be one of the most popular big game animals harvested.

In warm weather, deer should be skinned and quartered ASAP.

Some things consistently make venison really tasty, but some things will ruin the flavor. Here are the worst offenders:

Poor field care. In the real world of hunting, things happen. We all make bad shots on occasion. And while we know not to push a deer that's been hit marginally, realize that the longer it takes for the animal to die and the farther it runs, the more adrenaline and lactic acid buildup in the animal's system and muscles. This is another reason to wait a few minutes before you get down from your stand to track the animal. The faster a deer hits the ground and can be field-dressed, the better the meat will be. Some of the best-tasting deer I've ever had have been shot in the head with a gun. The animal is killed instantly, and the meat is uncontaminated by blood and entrails from the chest cavity. That said, headshots are risky. The lungs and heart remain the best place to aim.

Failure to quickly cool. Internal bacteria rapidly take over after death, expelling gases and causing the animal to bloat. That's the first step in decomposition. This process is accelerated in warm weather. Field dressing and removing those organs are the first steps in cooling the animal down. I will use a stick to keep the rib cage open and snow, if possible, to help get the critter cooled. If the weather is in the mid-30s or lower, a deer can be left hanging skin-on overnight. In especially cold weather, my hunting buddies and I like to age a deer this way for several days.

Shot granddaddy Bullwinkle. Most hunters are in tune with herd management. Working with the fish cops (DNR), my hunting buddies have learned the practices that contribute to the health of a herd, including which deer to shoot. Given the chance, most of us want to shoot a mature buck with big antlers—me included. Big old bucks are perfectly edible but rarely the best. Muscles get tougher with use and stringy with age. An old buck that's spent a full autumn fighting, rubbing, scraping, and chasing does will be lean. Expect chewy steaks. Same goes for an old doe that's burned all her summertime calories producing milk to nurse fawns. I usually make deer burger, sausage, and jerky out of these critters. For steaks, you can't beat a young, crop-fed deer. Deer that spend a summer munching on corn and soybeans have an easier life—and more fattening food sources—than those that spend a lifetime wandering the big timber in search of scattered mast and browse.

Didn't age. If the mercury rises above 50 degrees, that's too warm to let a deer hang, so quartering and icing a deer down is the only option. We line the bottom of large coolers with a layer of ice, add the deer quarters on top of that, and then cover them with more ice. We keep the coolers in the shade with the drain plug open and on a downhill incline. That's very important. The idea is to let the ice slowly melt and drain from the coolers. This not only keeps the meat cold but purges an amazing amount of blood from it. We do this for at least two days, checking the ice a couple times per day in especially warm weather. (Note: If you do this without a drain plug, you'll get the opposite effect—deer quarters that are essentially marinated in bloody, dirty water.)

Dirty power saws and cutting tools. A deer's legs are held together just like yours: with ball-and-socket joints and connective tissue. Learn where these are, and you can cut an entire skinned deer apart within minutes with a good knife. Laying into a deer's legs and spine with a power saw puts bone marrow, bone fragments, and whatever mess was on the saw blade into your meat. I keep several sharp knives handy when I'm cleaning a deer. One is for field dressing. This one will be a stout knife with a drop point for prying through bone. Another is for skinning. A skinning blade with a gut hook is the best way to go. These knives can be honed to a razor's edge and quickly re-sharpened. Other than quickly dulling a knife's edge by slicing through hair, skinning is not taxing on a knife's blade, so a flexible fillet knife also works fine. Finally, I swap over to another knife—again, with a heavier blade—for quartering. Another point to remember is to keep your knives separate so you reduce the chances of contaminating the meat with blood and hair.

Forgot to trim the fat. Unlike beef fat, deer fat does not taste good. Neither do the sinew, membranes, and other connective tissues holding the various muscle groups together. Venison, whether destined for steaks or hamburger, should be trimmed free of anything that's not rich, red meat.

Needed more fat for grinding. Because fat needs to be trimmed away for the meat to have the best flavor, venison often becomes too lean for hamburger purposes. Patties made for grilled double cheeseburgers often fall apart soon after hitting the hot grate. The solution is to add some fat, either beef or pork, when you're grinding venison. We use cheap bacon, mixed at a rate of 5:1 (5 pounds of venison per pound of bacon). It makes our patties stick together, and the bacon adds a great flavor. We also will use cheap hamburger from the market, 60 to 70 percent lean, to add flavor.

Used a cut-rate butcher shop. Some commercial deer processors do a great job. But some do not. I once took a deer to a butcher, filled out my paperwork, and watched him disappear to the freezer room. He weighed my animal and returned with a corresponding amount of packaged, frozen venison. "We mix all our meat together and package a lot of burger at once," he said. For all I knew, the deer I was getting could've been gut-shot and left to hang in 90-degree heat. Insist on getting your own deer back when you have processing work done. If that's not possible, do it yourself. You will be glad you did.

Poor packaging and freezing. Freezer burn doesn't help the flavor of ice cream or anything else, including deer meat. We package our deer the old-fashioned way, first wrapping the portion in clear plastic wrap, and then covering that with heavy-duty freezer paper. Each package is clearly labeled, so we know the cut of meat, when it was killed, and also which deer it came from. If one animal proves especially tough, we know to use that meat for slow-cooking recipes.

Cooking for Man's Best Friend

A few months ago, while we were hunting pheasants, one of my buddies asked me what I feed my chocolate lab, Captain Bly. I told him, of course, that I make the Captain's dog food myself. Later that night he texted me asking for a couple of my dog food recipes so he could start making his labs and hounds their own custom food. Long story short, I've found that most hunters are like me—they love making their own dog food! This way, they know what Old Yeller is really eating. I have found that Captain Bly is a lot healthier eating the food Daddy makes for him, so as a special bonus, here are several of Captain Bly's favorite foods, including homemade doggie treats.

THE CAPTAIN'S BIG BOY CASSEROLE

2 cups converted long-grain white rice	¼ teaspoon garlic powder
2 teaspoons safflower oil	2 cubes beef bouillon
2 cups water	1 pound deer burger
¼ teaspoon ground thyme	1 cup grated Monterey Jack cheese

Combine rice and safflower oil in a saucepan over medium heat; stir and cook 2 minutes. Add the water, thyme, garlic powder, and bouillon. Cover, and cook for 15 minutes over medium heat, or until liquid is absorbed. Meanwhile, cook the deer burger in a large skillet over medium heat until browned, about 10 minutes. Drain, then stir into the rice along with the Monterey Jack cheese until the cheese melts. Make sure to cool completely before serving.

HUNTING POOCH SWEET TATER TREATS

1 sweet potato

2½ cups whole-wheat flour

¼ cup unsweetened applesauce

2 eggs

Preheat oven to 350 degrees. Prick sweet potato several times with a fork. Cook sweet potato in a microwave on high until tender, about 6 minutes. Cut potato in half, and scoop flesh out of the skin into a bowl; discard skin. Mash potato with a fork or potato masher, and transfer about 1 cup to a large bowl. Save any remaining sweet potato for another use. Mix whole-wheat flour, applesauce, and eggs in the large bowl with the sweet potato until a dough forms. Turn dough out on a well-floured surface, and roll to about ½-inch thick. Cut out shapes using a cookie cutter, or cut dough into strips with a pizza cutter. Arrange cookies on an ungreased baking sheet. Bake until crisp, 35 to 45 minutes. Cool in the pans for 10 minutes before removing to cool completely on a wire rack.

HE'S A GOOD BOY DOGGY VITTLES

6 cups water

1 pound ground turkey meat (I never waste wild game!)

2 cups brown rice

1 teaspoon dried rosemary

½ package frozen broccoli, carrots, and cauliflower combination

Place the water, ground turkey, rice, and rosemary into a large Dutch oven. Stir until the ground turkey is broken up and evenly distributed throughout the mixture. Bring to a boil over high heat, then reduce heat to low and simmer for 20 minutes. Add the frozen vegetables, and cook for an additional 5 minutes. Remove from heat, and cool. Refrigerate until using.

DADDY'S BUDDY BIRTHDAY AND HOLIDAY FEAST

2 chicken leg quarters

1 cup brown rice

1 pound ground venison

2/3 cup rolled oats

1 package frozen chopped spinach, thawed and squeezed dry

2 cups frozen chopped broccoli, thawed

1 can kidney beans, rinsed, drained, and mashed

2 carrots, shredded

1 clove garlic, minced (optional)

1 cup cottage cheese

½ cup olive oil

Place the chicken leg quarters in a large pot, and fill with enough water to cover by 1 inch. Bring to a boil, then reduce heat to medium-low, cover, and simmer 40 minutes. Remove the legs, and allow to cool. Strain and return the cooking liquid to the pot. Once the legs have cooled, remove and discard the skin and bones; chop the meat, and set aside. Stir the brown rice into the reserved chicken broth, and bring to a boil. Reduce heat to medium-low, cover, and simmer until the rice is tender, 45 to 50 minutes. Drain off any excess liquid, and add the rice to the bowl with the chicken. Heat a large skillet over medium-high heat, and add the ground venison. Cook and stir until the deer meat is crumbly and no longer pink, about 7 minutes. Pour off any excess grease, and place the deer meat into the bowl. Stir in the oats, spinach, broccoli, kidney beans, carrots, garlic, cottage cheese, and olive oil. Store the dog food in resealable containers in the freezer. Thaw the daily portions overnight in the refrigerator. Your hunting pal will love this feast!

HUNTING CABIN BREAKFAST DOG BISCUITS

1 egg

1/3 cup peanut butter

½ cup mashed banana

1 tablespoon honey

1 cup whole wheat flour

½ cup wheat germ

1 egg white, lightly beaten, for brushing

Preheat oven to 300 degrees. Lightly grease a baking sheet. Stir together the egg, peanut butter, banana, and honey in a medium bowl; blend thoroughly. Stir in the flour and wheat germ; mix well. Turn dough out onto a floured board, and roll to ¼ inch thick. Cut into desired shapes with a cookie cutter, place on prepared baking sheet, and brush tops with egg white. Bake biscuits in oven until dried and golden brown, about 30 minutes, depending on size. Remove from oven, and cool on a wire rack.

RECIPE INDEX

RECIPE INDEX

RECIPE INDEX

RECIPE INDEX

RECIPE INDEX